SPALDING®

WINNING SOCCER

Jerry Yeagley

A Division of Howard W. Sams & Company
A Bell Atlantic Company

Published by Masters Press
(A Division of Howard W. Sams & Company, A Bell Atlantic Company)
2647 Waterfront Pkwy. E. Drive, Suite 100
Indianapolis, IN 46214

Published 1994

        96 97 98 99   10 9 8 7 6 5 4

Printed in the United States of America

Library of Congress Cataloging-in-Publication Data

Yeagley, Jerry.
    Winning soccer / Jerry Yeagley.
          p.   cm. (Spalding sports library)
        ISBN: 0-940297-96-7
        1. Soccer -- Training.   2. Soccer -- Coaching. I. Title. II. Series.
GV943.9.TY44   1994   94-13401
796.334'07--dc20   CIP

Editor: Mark Montieth

*Cover photograph by Rick Notter. All other photographs by Kent Phillips,
except on page vi, which was provided by the Sports Information Depart-
ment at Indiana University.*

Fitness illustrations by Rita Powell.

To Barney Hoffman, my high school coach, and Mel Lorback, my college coach — men who taught me about life as well as soccer.

and

To Bill Armstrong, whose friendship and unyielding support helped make Indiana soccer what it is today.

Contents

Preface

In 1963, soccer was barely a rumor at Indiana University. A club team had been allowed to participate for several years, but it was no more than a recreational outlet for interested students. The university provided little funding, and offered no scholarships.

Today, Indiana has perhaps the best collegiate program in the nation. It has won three NCAA championships, has competed in the Final Four nine times and plays in its own state-of-the-art stadium.

What happened in the meantime?

Jerry Yeagley.

No college team in the United States bears the imprint of one person as much as Indiana's soccer team does. After taking over as coach of the club team in 1963, Yeagley fought for 10 years to have it elevated to a varsity sport. After that battle was won, he wasted no time turning it into one of the elite programs in the country. By 1976, the Hoosiers were competing for the national championship. In 1982, they won the first of their three titles. Throughout the 1980s they won more games and had the best winning percentage (.813) of any team in the nation. They remain a national power today.

If that sounds like a Cinderella story it's nothing new for Yeagley, who's been handy with a glass slipper throughout his soccer career. Back in tiny Myerstown, Pa, where he was one of just 47 kids in his high school graduating class, Yeagley helped lead his team to the state championship, upsetting a much larger school in the final game. At West Chester State, a small Pennsylvania college, he helped lead his team to the NCAA championship in 1961, upsetting heavily-favored St. Louis University in the final game.

After completing work on his Master's Degree at the University of Pittsburgh in 1963, Yeagley was ready for new challenges. He had offers to take over established programs in the East, but he spotted another Cinderella-in-waiting in Bloomington, Ind. Indiana University was no Myerstown High School or West Chester State as far as its size, but its soccer program was as humble as it could be. Build a soccer power in the heart of Big Ten football country? To Yeagley's way of thinking, it seemed like "a neat thing to do."

Yeagley experienced a culture shock when he arrived at Indiana. Soccer was virtually unknown to most sports fans in the Midwest then. Most sporting goods stores didn't even sell soccer balls. Few high schools fielded teams. At Yeagley's first call-out for practice at I.U., eight players showed up, and they were most interested in knowing what trips the team would be taking so they could plan their parties accordingly. Yeagley remembers telling a woman at a restaurant during one of Indiana's early road trips that the group of young men before her were a soccer team. "Oh, soccer!" she said. "That's the game you play on horses, isn't it?"

Amid that environment of apathy and ignorance, Yeagley built his program from scratch. He grabbed the equipment the varsity sports were discarding. His players hung sheets on campus to publicize the games. As a group they lined the field, administered first aid and drove to the road games in their own cars, stopping at the homes of parents for meals along the way. Anything to save a few pennies.

Gradually, a program began to take shape. Competing against club teams and what few varsity programs existed in the Midwest then, Yeagley's teams won immediately. His first team went 5-1-3. The second finished 8-1-1. The third 9-1. Still, members of the university's administration at the time told Yeagley he was wasting his time trying to gain varsity status for an oddball sport such as soccer, and encouraged him to take a job at another school where the prospects were brighter.

But he stayed. And won. In 1973, amid growing pressure from the student body, community and a few university officials, soccer was granted varsity status. Although he had no scholarships at first, Yeagley at least had more funding and the blessings of the athletic administration. Finally armed with a launching pad, he fueled the takeoff.

His teams still soar today. In 21 years of varsity competition under Yeagley, the Hoosiers have won 359 games while losing just 66 and tying

32. They have competed in the NCAA tournament all but three of those years. Each one of his recruiting classes has competed for the national championship at least once.

Amid the team success, the individual honors have been many. Indiana has had 22 All-Americans, four Olympians, 36 professionals, 14 national team players, three national collegiate Players of the Year and three World Cup players. More than 20 of Yeagley's former players and assistants have become college coaches.

Yeagley too is well-decorated. He is the only person to be named Division I Coach of the Year twice. He has been inducted into the Pennsylvania Athletic Hall of Fame. And, in 1989, he received the highest honor of all: induction into the National Soccer Hall of Fame.

Indiana's soccer program has come a long way — from outcasts to champions. Another coach at Indiana who has won three national championships, basketball coach Bob Knight, has recognized Yeagley's rare accomplishments.

"There are a lot of good coaches who have been able to develop good programs in various sports where there is a foundation for that particular sport," Knight once said. "However, very, very few have been able to create something where there is no foundation.

"There is no valid reason why Indiana should have a great soccer team, yet Jerry has created a team that is nationally competitive and has been able to build a tradition where before there was absolutely none. What he has done is a unique and singular accomplishment for him as a coach. As I study college sports, I don't believe anyone, in any sport, at any school, has done what he has done with the soccer program here."

Throughout all the victories and all the honors, Yeagley has not lost sight of the reasons for his success. He realizes that the same fundamental skills and strategies that enabled his early teams to win are just as important today. This book — a compilation of Yeagley's successful previous books, *Soccer Skills* and *Soccer Strategies* — presents the gamut of the knowledge he has gained in more than 30 years of coaching winners.

THE EDITORS

Part I:
Individual Skills

Offense

No matter how much athletic talent your soccer team has, a mastery of the fundamentals is essential. A good place to start is with basic ball-handling skills.

Remember, your team's ability to score goals relies on first winning the ball, and then controlling it to create scoring opportunities. The game ultimately breaks down into its essential form — one-on-one battles all over the field — and in that domain, ball control rules.

Ball control is the foundation from which you build your individual soccer skills. All techniques and strategies are based on a player's ability to handle the ball confidently and constructively, even under extreme pressure. Your ultimate goal is to feel so at ease with the ball that it becomes an extension of your body. This can only be acquired through hours of dedicated practice.

Ball control revolves around the concept of "touch," the player's sense of feel and control. It must be developed from head to toe and it must become second nature so that you can assess your position and situation and make a confident decision quickly. If your mind is preoccupied with controlling the ball, you will not be able to make the correct decision quickly enough.

Occasions will arise during a game in which you can play the ball immediately, either by a pass, a shot, an interception or clearance. It is more common, however, to have to bring the ball under control before making a move. The more touches you must make to bring the ball under control, the more time a defender has to react and the more difficult it will be to make an effective move. Today's game, at the higher levels, is played at such a fast pace that you will not be able to create space for yourself and your teammates if you have poor ballhandling skills.

The good news is that a soccer ball is "user friendly." It is round and makes predictable bounces, unlike a football or rugby ball. After you become confident in your ballhandling skills the ball becomes an ally rather than an enemy, and you look forward to receiving it.

The only way to achieve this level, however, is through hours of practice. Even at the college level, players should work on their ballhandling skills year-round. At Indiana, we include at least 15 minutes of individual ball control work at each practice session.

The coach's responsibility toward improving players' ballhandling skills is to create an environment that enables all players to reach their maximum potential. This means providing the best possible training facilities and well-organized, disciplined practice sessions.

The coach also must motivate and guide the players through their development. This includes analyzing performance, providing appropriate demonstrations and demanding that all players follow the proper mechanical principles involved with every aspect of soccer technique.

The player's responsibility is total dedication to hard work and a willingness to put in the training time necessary to develop maximum potential. Playing beautiful, technically sound soccer is an art form, like playing the piano or golf. A person does not become a great golfer or a pianist without tireless hours of individual practice. The same holds true for a soccer player. What is your potential? Find out! Do not cheat yourself and your teammates by asking yourself after your playing days are over, "I wonder just how good I could have been?"

This section explores some of the fundamentals of ball control, and presents basic drills players can use to refine their skills.

Juggling

No one ever won a game by juggling the ball from one end of the field to the other. Juggling, however, is an essential element of ball control, and can make the difference between success and a missed opportunity. Controlling the ball in the air using various body parts is simply a method of gaining mastery over the ball and making it go where you want it to go. You develop touch and balance, which always are important in game situations.

Some players have been known to juggle a ball more than 12,000 times without letting it hit the ground. You do not need to worry about attempting such a feat, but it shows what is possible through practice. It is a good idea to keep track of your personal record and challenge yourself to surpass it. Juggling for long periods of time also helps develop your concentration and stamina, which are crucial in a game.

It is best to initiate juggling practice by lifting the ball with your foot. The easiest and most common lifting method is to stand about a foot away from the ball, put your foot on top of the ball, roll it back with the toe pointed downard, and then insert the foot under the ball so that it rests momentarily on the shoelaces, from where it can be lifted.

A more complicated lift is the scissors lift, in which you put your feet on each side of the ball and bring them together, causing the ball to rise. The

Juggling tips

- Check the ball for correct air pressure, and make sure your shoelaces are tied at the heel or on the outside of your foot.
- Find the center of the ball, whatever its size or weight, and meet it with the appropriate force of your foot, thigh, forehead or chest.
- Concentrate fully.
- Use your arms to maintain balance, and don't try to knock the ball up too high.

twister is similar, except the feet are crossed and then brought together to lift the ball up to get a foot under it. These are just a few examples. You should develop your own lifting tricks, then practice them until they become second nature.

After lifting the ball, keep it airborne with the insteps of your feet to start, alternating left and right, then proceed up your body incorporating your thighs, chest, shoulders and head. Your body should be loose and well-balanced, slightly crouched, with your weight on the ball of the supporting foot. Keep the body part you are using parallel to the ground and make your contacts gentle. Concentrate on making contact with the center of the ball.

Keep the ball under control as much as possible while gradually increasing your speed and the number of touches. Find and develop a rhythm, and then add movement to the exercise by walking forward, backward and sideways.

When using the instep to juggle, keep your toe pointed and concentrate on avoiding spin. When juggling on the thigh, avoid hitting the knee. For the head, chest and shoulders, maintain your body directly under the ball. Your forehead should be parallel to the ground, and your back arched for chest and shoulder juggling.

Juggling exercises are limited only by your imagination. Challenge yourself and have fun with the ball. Remember to work on your "weak" foot or thigh as much or more than your strong one so that you are equally adept with both.

Practice activities

Juggling can be practiced alone more easily than any other skill. All you need is a ball and a little open space.

Put the ball into play by dropping it from your hands or lifting it with your foot, then try to keep it from hitting the ground using various parts of your body, except of course the arms and hands. Don't be discouraged; it is more difficult than some players make it look. Start with perhaps five touches and build up the number gradually.

Functional juggling is an exercise to help you practice these techniques in a more game-like situation. Begin by lifting the ball, then juggling it low several times. On a given signal, kick the ball high into the air and attempt to control it using various parts of the body. Jumping to receive the ball adds more of a challenge.

Adding partners to your work will sharpen your reaction time and accelerate your development. When practicing with a friend or teammate, make up games to keep it fun and challenging. Conduct contests to see who can keep the ball in the air the longest. As you progress, see who can move from one point to another the fastest without letting the ball hit the ground.

2

Dribbling

Dribbling is the art of controlling the ball while moving at varying speeds and directions, using a sequence of soft touches with the inside, outside, toes and even the soles of both feet. It is not an end unto itself, however. It is a means to an end, namely passing to a teammate or shooting.

Advanced players must learn to dribble well enough that the ball appears to be glued to their foot, or at least tied to the foot by a string. The ball must become an extension of your body, so natural that you barely think about it as you advance it. This enables you to keep your head up and survey the field as you move, spotting open teammates for passes or potential scoring opportunities.

Dribbling skills are at the heart of winning the crucial one-on-one conflicts in a soccer game from the attacking player's perspective. If you can beat your defender with your dribbling, you create space for yourself by putting him behind you, and for your teammates by drawing other defenders toward you. A team that dominates one-on-one confrontations constantly puts the defense in jeopardy and increases its scoring opportunities. Ballhandling skills, particularly when enhanced by fakes, can make up for a lack of athleticism.

A team that has poor dribbling skills, however, puts itself in constant jeopardy. The attacking players tend to group together to help the ball

Dribbling tips

- Keep your head up as much as possible.
- Maintain balance so you can move in any direction when challenged by an opponent.
- Keep the ball within playing distance of your foot, and shield it from the opponent with your body.
- Try to keep the defender off-balance by a series of fakes.
- Vary your pace to keep the defender off balance and away from the ball.

handler and avoid a turnover. They are reluctant to make runs to receive passes because they feel they should remain nearby for a short pass or to defend if possession is lost. Defenders, meanwhile, become more confident and aggressive. The end result is a timid offense that has difficulty advancing the ball, and a nearly impossible time scoring.

Dribbling as a component of a team's offensive attack has gone in and out of style over the years. Some teams from some countries in certain eras have emphasized passing as much as possible. Other teams, however, such as in Brazil, have featured it as a part of their offensive attack. Regardless of how much it is emphasized, dribbling is crucial to every team's success.

Obviously, passing the ball is preferable to dribbling in most situations. The fastest dribbler in the world cannot move the ball faster than a sharp pass moves it. Dribbling is the best option in certain instances, however, such as when you need to:

- Confuse the defense and create scoring opportunities
- Advance the ball across open areas when a pass is not available
- Maintain possession of the ball when no passes are available
- Beat a defender between you and the goal

First, of course, you must master the basic dribbling techniques. Practice dribbling slowly at first, with an emphasis on keeping the ball under control, and then gradually build to full speed.

Keep in mind that you will not always want to dribble at full speed during games, particularly if you are not an advanced player. You can control the ball more effectively while dribbling slowly, and your passes are likely to be more accurate. You also allow yourself the option of accelerating quickly to elude a defender. Reserve dribbling at fast speeds for breakaway situations when you are in the open field.

At first you should remain crouched slightly over the ball and concentrate on getting a feel for it. Leaning over the ball helps keep it closer to your feet, instead of pushing it ahead and then running to catch up. Keep your weight on the balls of your feet; this enables you to make feints and changes of direction to get by a defender.

After you become comfortable dribbling on your own, practice against a defender. You will soon realize the need for developing skills with both feet, because you must screen the defender with your body and carry the ball with the outside foot. Wingers in particular must be skilled at screening, because they are often hemmed in by the touch lines or the corners of the field.

During games, if you beat a defender while heading toward the goal, move back in his path. This causes the defender to have to change his stride and allows you a clear path forward. You can practice this maneuver with a friend.

A great deal of practice time should be devoted to basic one-on-one confrontations to help players develop instincts for driving toward goal. During games, players should attack defenders directly, rather than trying to avoid them by moving around them — that only makes their job easier. Players should have the attitude, "I've got the ball and I'm going to beat you."

While it is good to have a wide variety of moves with the ball that can help you elude a defender, one good move is all that is really needed, particularly for younger players. If you study the game's great players, you see most of them have perfected one move and perhaps a counter to it. Everyone might know the move, but few if any can stop it. Select one move and concentrate on perfecting it. If you can do that, begin working on another.

Keep in mind that it is not always best to dribble toward the goal. That's the preferred course of attack, naturally. If you have an advantage over the defense, such as a two-on-one breakaway, you should head toward the goal. The same applies if you have an open field in front of you with no downfield passing options, or if you have just one defender to beat for a shot on goal.

Soccer at higher levels, however, is too complex to be able to move the ball toward the goal in a straight line. Think of the defense as a fence. Sometimes it is best to go over or through it, but sometimes it is best to back up and go around it.

You often will want to dribble across the field. This is more difficult to defend than dribbling straight ahead, and can serve several purposes. You can do it to create space when you don't believe you can beat a defender one-on-one, to set yourself up for a better shot on goal, to confuse the defense, or to buy time while your teammates move into a better scoring position.

Less often, but on occasion, you will want to move backward with the ball to avoid pressure, set yourself up to pass to a teammate or draw the defense away from their positions and create space around the goal for a potential pass.

Part of your dribbling skill should be knowing when *not* to dribble. Too often, inexperienced players lower their head and charge toward the goal after gaining possession of the ball. It usually is better to stop the ball, survey the field and then pass. (More advanced players should know exactly what to do with the ball by the time they receive it.)

This enables you to keep space between you and the defense and buys time for you and your teammates to create passing options. The player who can draw the attention of more than one defender and then make an effective pass to a teammate is of much more value than the player who gets past three defenders with his dribbling but then loses the ball to the fourth. The best dribblers know when to pass the ball.

Your decisions while dribbling will depend partially on your position on the field. You rarely would want to challenge a defender in your own penalty area, or in your defensive third of the field, because a mistake could lead to a shot on goal. If you are near the opponent's goal, however, you can afford to challenge a defender and take a chance. You might set yourself up for a shot on goal, and if you lose possession your teammates have an opportunity to cover for you defensively.

The touch line areas of the field in the offensive third also offer an opportunity to challenge the opponent. Many goals come from players who beat their opponents on the wings and then create a scoring opportunity for themselves or a teammate. Skilled players can make exceptions to these guidelines, but should be careful. The consequences of ill-advised dribbling can be serious.

The ability to pass while dribbling requires that you have your head up. By doing so, you signal your teammates that you are prepared to pass, and therefore keep them alert and active. You also avoid defensive pressure, because the defenders have to be prepared for a pass. If you dribble with your head down, you invite the defense to pursue you and turn your teammates into spectators. The point cannot be emphasized enough: Keep your head up as much as possible while dribbling.

It also is important to keep the ball within a comfortable playing distance, so that you can quickly change pace and direction. On a breakaway you will want to push the ball ahead of you to gain speed, but most of the time you want to keep it close, as if it were attached to a string tied to your ankle.

• • •

An important part of your ballhandling skill as you progress should be fakes, or feints. They can accomplish many things for you, such as:

- Beating a defender
- Forcing the defense to back off
- Confusing or intimidating the defense
- Creating opportunities for yourself or your teammates

The fake you execute will depend on the situation. If the defender is marking you too aggressively, a false start will throw him off balance. If you can move either left or right, fake one way and go the other. If the defense is set up for a pass, fake a pass and then dribble.

Fakes should become automatic and intuitive. Like anything, however, they can be overdone. To fake all the time is to be like the boy who cried wolf. The defense will no longer be fooled. By mixing fakes into your ballhandling, you will keep the defense off balance and create opportunities for yourself.

Fakes are most effective when the defender is marking you aggressively. Of course it is more difficult to execute one under pressure, but an effective fake will help prevent the defender from pursuing you aggressively in the future. They can neutralize an entire defense.

A fake can be as simple as leaning one way with the head and shoulders and going the other. The legs do not shift, so you are not likely to lose possession. Another effective, more advanced fake, is to step over the top of the ball. This can be done to simulate a pass, false start, change of direction or shot.

• • •

A more intricate method of ball control, one that is often incorporated with fakes, is to use the sole of the foot to move the ball. This technique is more advanced and is considered a bit flashy for beginning players, but it can be an effective means of eluding a defender. It is similar to dribbling a basketball behind your back: it is effective when it works, but you can look foolish if you lose possession.

Some players roll the ball with the sole of the foot to set up a pass or a shot on goal, but generally it is done to beat a defender in close quarters. It can aid in shifting direction quickly, and can be used while shielding the ball and considering your options. This skill should be used as part of a greater strategy, such as setting up a pass or shot, or as part of a fake. It is of no use unless it takes the ballhandler somewhere.

You must work to develop touch with the bottom of your foot just as you do with the rest of your foot. This is a precise skill that requires sureness of touch and good balance. It is often employed by players who favor a "strong" foot, as a means for covering up their weak side.

A simple method of practicing this technique is by rolling the ball along a line, either straight or curved, and then stopping at various intervals to pull it back with the bottom of the foot. Make the move more quickly as you progress, and incorporate it with a shift of direction. Practice rolling the ball from the bottom of your foot to the instep to move forward again. This technique must be executed quickly to be effective in game situations.

• • •

An even more intricate and flashy maneuver is to push the ball between your opponent's legs, usually with an inside-of-the-foot pass, and catch it on the other side. This move is often called the "nutmeg."

This maneuver is to be used only rarely, and must be done instinctively when the opportunity presents itself. It carries with it the responsibility of showmanship, meaning you must be aware that it can anger and motivate the defender who is made to look foolish. On the other hand, it can provide a psychological weapon for the offense.

The basic version of the maneuver occurs when the defender assumes a low, wide stance in front of you. If he is too close to you, the opportunity presents itself to slide the ball between his legs and recover it on the other side. This can occur when you are dribbling quickly toward a stationary defender, or when a defender approaches you too quickly. You also can induce him to take such a stance by changing direction several times as you approach him.

You also can execute this maneuver between the legs of a moving defender, but this is even more difficult and instinctive. If the defender runs across from the side and commits himself, you can scoot the ball between his legs as his momentum carries him past you.

These moves obviously are risky. If you are inaccurate with your pass between the defender's legs, or if he recovers in time to intercept it, you are doing nothing more than passing the ball to the defense.

These maneuvers can be practiced with a friend, but again they are primarily instinctive moves against an opportunity that presents itself randomly throughout a game.

• • •

Good players must be able to withstand tackles through quickness or strength, or both. Every challenge calls for a slightly different approach, but some basic principles apply. Balance is essential. Quick reactions, both physically and mentally, are important as well. And you must be able to keep the ball from defenders, either by shielding the ball with a protecting leg or by running past the defender on the run.

These situations make clear the need to develop ballhandling skills with both of your feet, because you obviously cannot control which side the defenders attack from.

Practice activities

Dribbling can be practiced on your own, of course. More advanced players, however, should practice against a defender as often as possible to simulate game situations. Focus on control. Practice at high speeds only after you are comfortable at slower speeds.

Drills such as the step-up, roll-over and pendulum are good for beginners to find the "glue" they need to control the ball in game situations. In the beginning you will want to watch the ball, but as you progress make it a point to keep your head up and maintain proper balance by staying on the balls of your feet.

With the step-up, keep the ball as still as possible on the ground while making alternating touches with the balls of both your feet. Start slowly, then gradually increase the speed of your contacts. A reasonable goal is 100 touches in 30 seconds. As you improve, perform this activity while moving forward and backward.

Another good exercise for beginners is to practice rolling the ball along the ground by brushing the sole of your foot across the top of it, using your other foot to keep your body balanced. Roll it sideways, first one way and then the other, while moving laterally. Try it slowly at first, then add speed. Change feet to develop touch going both ways. As mentioned earlier, you won't use this skill in a game very often except over short distances to elude a defender or execute a fake. Still, practicing this skill helps develop your touch for the ball and does have its place in specific game situations.

The pendulum assists in improving various swerving moves while dribbling. Remain stationary at first, moving the ball lightly back and forth between the insides of the feet. Later add movement, going forward and backward while controlling the ball. Concentrate on keeping your hips loose and establishing a rhythm.

As you progress, make up your own exercises to improve your dribbling skills. You can gather several friends in a circle and dribble the ball within the group without looking at the ball. Change direction, weaving in and out of each other. You can place restrictions, such as using one foot only.

Advance by setting up an obstacle course with cones or poles or other objects that represent defenders, and dribbling through it. Use short, quick steps, striking the ball gently on every step, or every other step, to keep it close.

3

Passing

You kick the ball for two reasons: to shoot it or pass it. The vast majority of your kicks, however, will be passes.

On the average, players pass the ball about 80 percent of the time after receiving it during games. The only other options are to shoot it or dribble it. Shots are difficult to come by and dribbling is less preferred than passing. Therefore passing is the lifeline of a team, the skill that links the players into a cohesive unit rather than a bunch of scattered individuals. A team that passes poorly has no chance to mount a threatening offense.

You should pass the ball when you are in danger of losing it because of defensive pressure or when an open teammate is in a better position than you are. When in doubt, pass to the player with the most space available to him, even if he is alongside you or behind you.

More advanced players might be less inclined to practice passing, but its importance actually increases with each level of play. Skilled ballhandlers might be able to defeat an opponent at a low level of play, but never at an advanced level. As players become more athletic and skilled, passing becomes more difficult and crucial.

An endless variety of passes are available: short, long, low, high, hard, soft, forward, sideways, backward, with the inside of the foot, the outside, the instep, the heel or even the toe. Each is correct in certain situations.

17

Passing tips

- To keep the ball on the ground, strike the ball at its midline, or slightly above.
- To kick the ball into the air, strike it below the midline.
- Keep your eyes on the ball as you strike it.
- Keep your ankle firm and follow through with the foot to achieve power and accuracy.
- Keep the non-kicking foot next to the ball, pointing at the target.

Except for the position of the kicking foot, the principles are the same for all of them.

The non-kicking foot should be positioned beside the ball, with the toe pointed toward the target. Lean forward as you begin your kicking motion, so that your head and the knee of the kicking leg are over the ball as you strike it. Your eyes should be focused on the ball as you make contact, and the head should stay down as you follow through. The ankle should always be held firm.

Striking the ball below its center gives height to your kick, while hitting the center causes the ball to stay near the ground as it moves toward its target. The position of the non-kicking foot also is crucial because it provides balance. If the non-kicking foot is not in the correct position, you will not be able to generate maximum power.

• • •

The three primary elements of passing are accuracy, touch and timing.

Accuracy does not necessarily mean placing the ball at a teammate's feet, however. Passes on the ground are generally easier for your teammates to receive than passes in the air, but sometimes a pass should be delivered in front of a moving teammate, for example, or high enough for him to head the ball. You should know where your teammates like the ball to be placed and pass accordingly. Of course the receiving player has a responsibility in executing a good pass as well. He must be in the proper position, and have the skill to receive it cleanly.

If the receiving player has space, it usually is best to pass to his feet. If the receiving player is closely marked, it usually is best to pass to the space behind the defender. A player who lacks quickness probably prefers the ball to be placed near his feet, while a quick player probably wants the ball passed into an open space where he can run it down.

A receiving player can tip off the ballhandler by his positioning. If he wants the ball passed to his feet, he faces the passer. If he wants to receive the ball in an open area, he faces that area. This is all part of communication that develops with experience.

Touch — the force or speed of a pass — determines how easily the ball can be properly received. If it is too strong it will be difficult to control. If it is too weak it probably will be intercepted. A weak pass also can place your teammate in a precarious situation with a defender and leave him open to possible injury.

Timing — knowing when to release the ball — is more difficult and is learned primarily through game experience. It involves knowing the style, ability and intentions of your teammates.

A pass that lacks any of these three elements can, at the very least, throw your offense out of sync and spoil a scoring opportunity. More likely, it will lead to loss of possession.

Passing also includes other, more subtle, elements. You need good peripheral vision, which of course can only be used if your head is up. The ability to spot an open teammate in a crowded area of the field or on the blind side is a skill unto itself.

The element of surprise also comes into play. A back heel pass, for example, can catch a defense off guard, but so can a simple pass if you do not telegraph your intention.

All of these aspects of passing are secondary to learning the basic fundamentals of each type of kick.

• • •

The *inside of the foot* kick, or push pass, is the most elementary and common kick in soccer. Approximately 70 percent of the passes in a soccer game are of this variety. The inside of the foot presents the biggest contact surface with the ball, and therefore provides the best accuracy.

The kicking foot should be turned outward so that the inside portion of the shoe meets the ball squarely. The ankle must be held firm, with the toe pointed upward. Your non-kicking foot should be even with or slightly behind the ball so that the knee of your kicking leg is over the ball when your foot makes contact. With a moving ball you should position your support (non-kicking) foot slightly ahead of the ball so that when contact is made your delivery foot is over the ball at impact.

The primary advantage of this kick is that it is the most accurate. The disadvantages are that it is relatively easy for defenders to predict, and it is unsuitable for long or hard passes because it is more difficult to generate power. It also is a difficult pass to make while running at or near full speed because you must interrupt your stride.

Because it is used so frequently, this kick is a good one to learn first.

• • •

The *instep drive* is most powerful kick in soccer because the ball is struck with the shoe laces. It begins with a full swing from the hip and ends with a full follow-through with the toe pointed downward. If the toe is not down, you probably won't kick the ball cleanly. It is important to cock your knee back, as this is where you generate your power.

Remember to plant your support foot next to the ball and point it toward your target so that the knee of your kicking leg is directly over the ball at the instant of impact. Your head should be down and held steady, with your eyes focused on the ball. As you strike the ball, lock your knee and ankle and follow through. You should approach the ball at about a 30-degree angle.

The instep kick offers the advantage of distance and power. It can provide you with a potent shot on goal as an offensive player and a powerful clearance when on defense. It is easier to disguise your intentions with this kick, which makes it more difficult for the defense to predict its direction. This kick can be made while running at full speed without interrupting your stride.

The disadvantage of the instep kick is that it is more difficult to kick accurately because of the smaller surface of the foot used in the kick. A poorly struck ball can sail far from its intended direction.

The instep drive can be used for both low drive and lofted passes. The low drive is similar to a golfer's shot off the tee. The ball is struck with the instep at the center of the ball so that it remains close to the ground. The backswing and follow-through should be complete. Timing also is crucial. You are likely to get better distance and accuracy if you kick the ball in a controlled fashion rather than trying to kick the cover off the ball — a common mistake among younger players. A smooth, rhythmic motion is best.

The low drive from the instep has relatively limited use. You simply won't have that many opportunities during a game to pass the ball forward on the ground over a great distance without the defense intercepting. Most of the time, its use is limited to pass crossfield.

The lofted pass is much more common than the low drive; it obviously is easier to kick the ball over defenders than through them. Advanced players can kick the ball more than 50 yards. Keep in mind, however, that the ball will not have a steep trajectory on its "takeoff." Defenders standing within 10 yards or so might be able to deflect it before it reaches its full height.

To execute this pass, strike the ball slightly below its center with the front portion of the instep, where the big toe joins the body of the foot.

Your approach on this kick is crucial. The last step before kicking the ball should be longer than the rest and at a slight angle. The non-kicking foot should be placed to the side of the ball and slightly behind it. You want to pivot from the hips to produce more power and your body should lean backward slightly, but your motion should remain controlled.

This kick is more difficult than most for beginning players to master, particularly with a moving ball, but it can be done. Lack of proper execution rather than lack of strength usually prevents successful kicks. If you get adequate height but not distance, you probably are not following through properly. If you get too much height, you probably are striking the ball too low. If you kick the ball too low, you probably are striking the ball too high; perhaps you lifted your head before connecting with the ball.

The instep kicks are rather difficult to master, but they are worth the effort. One good one can lead directly to a scoring opportunity.

Other variations of the instep kick also are available.

The *jab pass* can be effective for use in tight quarters because it can be released quickly. The jab is similar to the instep drive, except the jab pass is a one-lever kick, meaning that no follow through is used.

The *pivot instep* is used to make long, lofting passes. It is most commonly used for kicks on goal, corner kicks and long clearances. The pivot instep technique differs somewhat from the instep drive, because the approach to the ball is from the side. The non-kicking or support foot is placed behind and to the side of the ball. This causes the kicker to lean back slightly, creating the loft of the ball.

The *chip pass* is used to place a short, lofted ball over an opponent. This can be effective in many situations. The chip pass is made by getting the instep of the kicking foot well under the ball and jabbing at it. The follow-through is shortened by lifting the knee after contact. The ball should have backspin which causes it to "stick" to the ground after landing, allowing it to be easily received by a teammate.

The non-kicking foot should be close to the ball and level with it. The supporting leg should be bent slightly at the knee. The approach is straight, with the kicking leg moving in a straight line in the direction you want the ball to travel.

The chip pass is not difficult, but it requires practice to place the ball exactly where you want it to go. A poorly hit kick is usually the result of being too far away from the ball when making impact, lifting your head or using the incorrect kicking motion.

The kick is easier to execute with a still ball or one that is rolling toward you and on a soft surface. It is much more difficult to perform on a hard surface with a ball rolling away from you, but it can be done.

The chip pass has become a greater weapon in recent years because of changes in modern defensive play, evolving from a fancy skill to a fundamental method of advancing the ball. It is effective because it can advance the ball over tight-marking opponents and allow time for your teammates to move into a position to receive the ball. In rare cases, it can be used for a shot on goal against a keeper who has strayed out of position.

• • •

The third-most common kick is the *outside-of-the-foot* kick. Used mainly as a flicking type of pass, it can be developed as a powerful adjunct to your kicking arsenal. This is a more advanced kick, and should be developed after a player has mastered the push pass and the instep kicks. This kick can be used for short and long passes, and for low or lofted passes.

When making a short pass, your foot should be positioned to the inside of the ball, with the toe pointed down and in. You then catch the ball with the outside of your foot as you rotate your foot in an outward motion. This kick requires a minimum of foot movement and is easy to disguise because you don't have to alter your running stride to execute it. It therefore is effective for bending passes down the line or setting up a give-and-go.

• • •

An effective pass for setting up shots on goal or for shots on goal, including corner kicks, is the *bender*, also known as the swerve pass or banana pass. It can be made with the outside or the inside of the foot. Follow through is important in either case.

When using the outside of the foot to make the kick, the foot comes across the body and strikes the ball from the outside toward the inside (for a right-footed kick), connecting with it just left of its center and near its middle. This places a spin on the ball and slices it to the right.

The non-kicking foot, for both long and short passes with the outside of the foot, should be positioned slightly behind and to the side of the ball to leave room for the kicking motion.

Artful execution of this pass can bend the ball around an opponent — including the goalie. It can be done at full speed without breaking stride. It is a difficult kick to control, however, and requires a great deal of practice. It also can be a difficult kick to receive because of its curving trajectory and spin. Because of these factors, it remains a relatively rare kick, one that should be reserved for special situations when a simpler pass will not be effective.

The inside of the foot also can be used to execute a swerve kick, and generally provides a bit more control than the outside of the foot. In this instance, the foot comes across the ball from the inside to the outside. The ball is struck by the front portion of the inside foot, near the joint of the big toe. Contact is made just right of center (for a right-footed kick), imparting a spin and swerve to the ball from right to left. Remember, in all bending passes, the ball will travel in the direction of the spin that you place on it.

• • •

The most rare, and probably the most difficult, pass in soccer is the backheel pass, which is delivered backward with the heel or sole of the foot. It has the element of ultimate surprise, but is difficult to execute accurately. It is a tool for the advanced player.

The kick can be used for three purposes: to retain possession in heavy traffic, to set up a teammate in a unique passing situation, or as a goal attempt. It usually is an instinctive reaction to a game situation. Still, it is the most appropriate pass for certain situations.

The most common application of this pass is near the middle of the field near your opponent's goal, when you are moving across the field with defenders in pursuit. By backheeling at the appropriate time, you can set up a teammate for a more direct pass or shot. Keep in mind, however, that while you probably will surprise your defenders, you also might surprise your teammates.

Above all, be extremely careful about attempting this pass near your own goal. You might wind up passing the ball into your own net, or making an unplanned "assist" to an opponent.

• • •

The *volley pass* is made on an airborne ball. It is obviously more difficult than kicking the ball off of the ground, but it is an important skill.

Volley passes can be made with the instep, or the inside or outside of the foot. The inside of the foot provides a large area for contact, and enables you to control the angle of your pass by altering the angle of your foot. Volley passes can be executed at almost any angle, high or low.

The outside of the foot volley leaves less margin for error. It is easily disguised, however, as you use primarily the same stance as you would a volley with the inside of the foot. Simply by turning the foot inward at the last moment, you can pass the ball in the direction opposite the one the

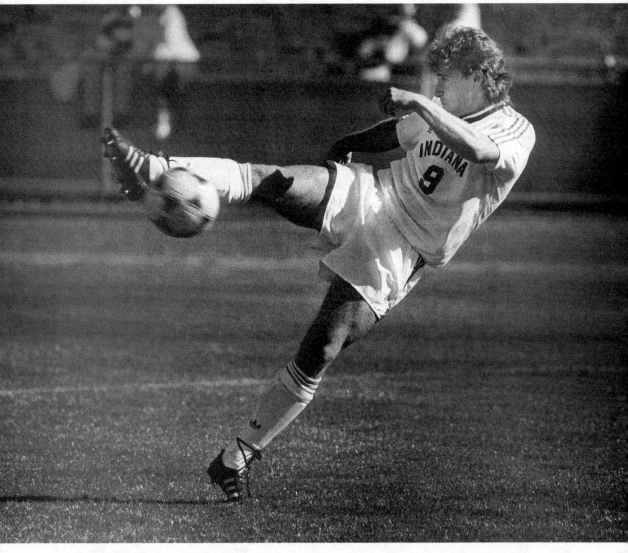

defense might be expecting. As you advance, it is important to learn to volley with both sides of the feet.

Mastering the volley passes enables you to become a "one-touch" player, increasing your efficiency greatly. Rather than having to receive the ball and get it under control before making your pass, you can pass it immediately. This keeps pressure on the defense and helps create scoring opportunities.

Volley passes require quick thinking and quick reactions. That doesn't mean, however, they must be hurried shots. An experienced player can develop the poise and sense of touch required to execute this pass and make it an effective weapon.

• • •

A *toe pass* is generally frowned upon and used only in extreme conditions for defenders or attackers around the goal. However, in the close confines of the indoor game, the "toe bash" provides quick release and high velocity. Important goals have been scored by the use of the toe in reaction situations.

• • •

The *through pass,* or forward pass, is the most productive pass because it penetrates the defense and moves the offense closer to the goal. It always is your first choice if it is available. Naturally, though, it is the most difficult to execute because the defense is set up to prevent it.

Generally a defender must be beaten for a player to be open for a through pass. Therefore it is often made to an open space, where an attacking player sprints to meet it, rather than directly to the player.

Through passes are often effective in starting combination plays. A pass is sent to an open space, drawing the defense. If your teammate can receive it, you or another teammate might be open in a scoring position.

The *square pass* neither advances nor retreats the ball, but can be quite effective. It spreads the defense and allows attackers more time to move into a scoring position. It also shifts the point of attack to another area of the field, where it might be more successful.

A square pass can be like a chess move: it doesn't accomplish much directly, but it sets up another, more effective move. It often precedes a through pass in a combination play, such as a give-and-go.

The *backward pass* is often misunderstood and under-utilized. The better soccer teams, however, use it frequently, as much as one-third of the time. Like the square pass, it can set up a through pass. Teammates behind you are more likely to be open, and have the best view of the playing area. They often can distribute the ball where it needs to go better than a player at midfield or beyond can.

Back passes create space downfield if the defense shifts to the ball, making it an effective means of setting up a penetrating pass. They also help a team consume time when it has a comfortable lead late in the game.

Naturally, the closer you are to the opponent's goal, the more viable a back pass becomes. Use it to retain possession when you are pressured or after you unexpectedly receive the ball from the opponent. It usually is a mistake to try to force the ball forward in the same area you receive it.

• • •

Passes made across the field, or *crosses*, are an integral part of almost any offense. Defenses generally try to force attackers to the flanks, away from the danger area in the middle of the field, to limit the options because the boundary line itself is a useful "defender." Yet it has been estimated that at least 60 percent of all goals are scored off of crossing passes or crossing shots on goal.

In earlier eras, crossing shots were thought to be a specialty for wingers, to get the ball to their teammates nearer the middle of the field. Today's more fluid offensive systems, however, demand that all players be able to make crossing passes.

Most crossing passes are made to players on the run or to open areas of the field. This requires not only kicking accuracy, but an acute sense of what is going on in other parts of the field. Crossing kicks ideally are placed so that another attacker can receive them on the run or in a position to shoot. They can be made low or high. Many of the goals scored on headers are the result of well-placed and well-timed crossing kicks.

Crosses are easier to execute when you have time and space. Look up, find your target area, adjust your body to suit the intended direction of the pass and stay relaxed. It is easy to tighten up when you spot a teammate in scoring position, but you are less likely to make an accurate kick if you are not relaxed.

Crossing passes, more than any other pass, must be made confidently. They must be made with just the right amount of force to reach their destination. A limp attempt that floats into a goalkeeper's hands or floats harmlessly over the end line can spoil a scoring opportunity and drain an attacking team's spirit. Swerve passes are a powerful ally in executing a crossing pass from a static position.

Crossing passes made on the run are much more difficult, but are more likely to break down a defense. The important element here is balance, as you are kicking the ball in a direction other than the one in which you are running. The placement of the non-kicking foot is crucial, and can only be learned through experience. It must be close enough to the ball to enable you to kick it with control, but far enough away to leave room for your sideways kicking motion. The more you are able to turn your body in the intended direction of the pass, the easier the kick becomes.

If you are making a right-footed cross, for example, your left foot would be placed slightly behind and to the left of the ball. Keep your arms, particularly the left, outstretched to provide balance, as if you were walking a tightrope. Keep your eyes on the ball and your head steady as you follow through.

Practice activities

Like nearly all soccer skills, these passes can be practiced alone. You can kick a ball against a wall, into a net, or back and forth with a partner. Begin with short kicks, concentrating on meeting the ball with the proper part of the foot, then increase your force and distance.

Learn the proper technique on a still ball, then work with a rolling ball, a dropping ball and a bouncing ball. You can shoot at targets if practicing alone. If working with a friend, work up to where you can pass to him while both of you are on the run.

4
Shooting

Ultimate success in soccer comes from scoring goals. Shooting, therefore, is the ultimate skill. Dribbling and passing skills are crucial to setting up shots on goal, but they do you no good if you can't put the ball in the net.

Coaches and players should be careful not to overlook this aspect of the game. With all the emphasis on the fundamentals of passing, dribbling and team play, scoring often is overlooked. Many times players have been taught to be unselfish and they wind up reluctant to shoot. Passing the ball is nothing more than passing the buck when you have a scoring opportunity. The great players have a genuine hunger to put the ball in the goal, and aren't afraid to take a chance now and then to do it. Coaches should encourage this approach among their players.

It is better to shoot and miss than let a good opportunity pass you by without shooting at all. This doesn't mean you should shoot wildly at the goal at every opportunity; that's a waste of energy and a disruption to your offense. You should, however, be aggressive in taking the ball to the goal. Don't be too concerned with over-shooting. Shooting itself, in fact, can lead to scoring opportunities. Many times a deflection off of the goalpost, the goalkeeper or someone else near the goal sets up the scoring kick.

Shooting tips

- All of the fundamentals of passing apply to shooting.
- Power and accuracy are equally important.
- Learn to shoot equally well with both feet.
- Most shots on goal during games are made on a moving ball, so practice sessions should be devised accordingly.
- Shooting practice should include a goalkeeper whenever possible.
- Shooters should follow their shots in practice, even in one-on-one activities, to get into the habit.

The Brazilians drove this point home with their great international success in the late 1950s and throughout the 1960s. Their "shoot on sight" mentality paid great dividends in helping them win championships in the World Cup and other international competition.

Virtually any kind of pass can be used in attempting a shot on goal, so the skills you acquire in practicing passing come into play here. I like to refer to shots, in fact, as passes that beat the goalkeeper.

Accuracy is the most important element of successful shots on goal, but power is an important factor as well. You should not blast the ball as hard as you can, but you do need to put force behind it, particularly on the longer shots. Your practice should reflect this requirement.

Most missed shots sail high over the goal, not wide. This comes from rushing the attempt and reaching too far with the last step, which leaves the support foot behind the ball. Perhaps the most important element of good finishing is to keep your head stationary and your eyes focused on the ball.

It might be natural to want to watch the ball as it lifts off, but just as in golf, if you lift your eyes away from the ball at the moment of contact you probably will top the ball or end up with a slice or a hook. The time to look up is before you strike the ball so that you can take aim. Once you shoot, you should not look up until you have connected with the ball and completed your follow through.

A mature psychological outlook also is important. You need to be able to shake off a missed shot and keep coming back. You cannot let it affect your confidence or your intensity. This means coaches and players alike should encourage players after missing a shot, as long as it was a reasonable attempt.

• • •

Of all the methods of kicking a ball into the goal — volleys, chip shots, lobs and so on — ground shots are by far the most common. Fortunately, they also are the easiest to execute. How many hours are you willing to devote to this skill? Not only will you sharpen your ability through practice, you also will boost your confidence, which will make you more aggressive in your approach to scoring.

Ground shots also are among the most difficult for the goalie to defend because it takes longer for him to drop down to stop a low ball than to reach up and stop a high one. The low shot also is more difficult for the goalie to see amid all the legs near the goal, and therefore is effective from greater distances when several bodies might be blocking the goalkeeper's vision.

Remember: Shoot often, and shoot low whenever possible.

Many goals are scored on one-touch shots. That's why it is so important to develop that skill, not only for passing, but for shooting. The advanced players can score on a one-touch shot from great distances. In the precious moments it takes you to gain control of the ball, a scoring opportunity can pass you by.

Your practice should reflect the relative need for power in your shooting. Closer shots obviously require less force, and in fact should emphasize accuracy. Longer shots require force to beat an alert defense, so your practice shots should be kicked that way.

Keep in mind, however, that the top scorers rarely shoot the ball with unnecessary force. The need for accuracy demands that you shoot with controlled power rather than brute force.

When receiving the ball close to the goal, you will find that your ability to control the ball with the inside of the foot will influence your success in scoring. Although power is a factor in shots from 10-15 yards out, your ability to sneak the ball past the goalkeeper is more important here. The inside of the foot often provides the best surface for controlling the ball in these situations.

• • •

Shots from difficult angles on the field obviously should be taken sparingly, but they have their place. The element of surprise is an important aspect of offense, and shots from the wide angles can stun an unsuspecting defense.

Some shots nearer the goal might be just as spectacular, such as the "scissors kick" or the diving header, but they are generally reactions to a situation when players are not in position to take a clean shot. An angled shot, however, is more a matter of choice — and sometimes it is a good choice.

These shots fall within the framework of a daring, confident approach to scoring. The players who take them must be sure of themselves and prepared to face criticism if and when they fail. After all, a teammate who hustles to get to an open scoring position won't look kindly on you if you attempt a difficult shot rather than cross the ball to him.

Difficult shots can succeed, however, and they stick in the memory when they do. They can boost the attacking team's confidence and hope, and demoralize the defense.

Your decision to attempt such shots should depend partly on the position of the goalkeeper. If he clearly is anticipating a pass and is not in position to stop an accurate shot, the time might be right to take it.

These shots can incorporate many of your passing skills. At times, a swerve pass might be needed to get the job done. At other times, you can kick the ball off the instep. Sometimes the inside of the foot kick will be the best method to get the ball by the goalkeeper.

Mastering the shots from difficult angles adds another powerful weapon to your offensive arsenal. You will become a less inhibited player and be far less predictable whenever you have the ball near the goal.

● ● ●

Swerving shots — the bending or banana kicks — can be taken from any angle. The ability to control the ball with this kick is almost essential in scoring from greater distances. In fact, it is difficult to shoot from long range without putting some swerve on the ball. Shooting the ball from a great distance along a straight line would be a difficult feat in itself. A swerving shot is a difficult shot to make with accuracy, however, even for the advanced players.

The kicking fundamentals are the same as for the swerving pass, but you must pay special attention to the ball's pace. The swerving shot made with the inside of the foot is likely to provide more control, while the shot taken with the outside of the foot should offer more power.

As you can imagine, a well-placed swerving shot on goal is difficult to stop. It is much like a curve ball in baseball. It is difficult to master, but even more difficult for the opposition to contend with. The best ones appear to be sailing away from the goal before curving back in.

• • •

Volleys, both high and low, are often necessary to score when you are near the goal. These kicks are usually an instant response to a pass, and made as one-touch shot attempts.

These shots are difficult because you have to hit a flighted ball exactly right, but like all difficult skills they can be highly effective.

The fundamentals of volley shots are the same as for passes. The most important factor is the placement of the non-kicking foot. It provides the balance necessary to execute the shot. Once placed, there is no turning back as you raise your leg to kick the ball. Many poorly hit volley shots are the result of improper placement of the non-kicking foot. This, again is a skill learned through experience.

Accuracy is a more important consideration than power with volleys. They are generally taken so close to the goal that a well-placed ball with any force at all will beat the goalkeeper. Trying to blast it past him will only compromise your accuracy. Power on a volley is determined by the amount of your leg swing. The lower the ball is received, the more powerful you will kick it. But by delaying the kick, you increase your chances of kicking it off your instep and sending it over the goal.

A more advanced form of volley is a lob over a goalkeeper or other defender. You place topspin on the ball so that it follows an arc, traveling over the defender and downward into the goal. In making this shot, you lean back and strike the upper portion of the ball with a jabbing motion. The kicking motion comes from the knee, and the ankle is locked with the toe pointed downward.

Higher volleys, made at waist level or above, are more difficult. They can be used by defenders to clear the ball or by wingers to send the ball to the middle of the field, but their most common use is for shots on goal. Most such volleys are a response to a crossing pass.

This shot requires a great deal of flexibility in the hips. Passes that are even with or slightly behind a player can be converted into shots on goal if he has the proper flexibility. The high volley is more a learned skill than a natural one, and a player's proficiency at it depends largely on his build. Such shots are usually an act of improvisation that require speed of thought and action.

To execute this shot, you must pick up the line of the ball's flight early and position your non-kicking foot accordingly. It will need to be placed as far from the ball as possible when making contact to enable you to fully extend your kicking leg. Do not lean too far backward, however, because you will lose balance and control. Keep your head still and your eyes focused on the ball. Make contact with your instep through the middle of the ball, or slightly higher. This is the difficult part; most missed high volley shots are the result of kicking the ball too low and sending it high over the goal. You should be able to make a corkscrew motion with the body as you kick the ball, swiveling 90 degrees or more as you follow through.

Again, you do not want to kick the ball too hard, as accuracy is more important. It is your speed in getting to the ball that counts, not the speed *of* the ball. Many chances are missed because players fail to set themselves up in time to make the shot. Proper positioning and rhythm will ensure the success of the shot more than power, although power is important in certain situations.

• • •

The overhead kick, also called the scissors kick or bicycle kick, is one of the most spectacular and difficult means of scoring, but it too has its place. It was perfected and popularized by Pelé, and has helped sell the game to fans and young players alike. Although it can be used by defenders to clear the ball and by wingers as a crossing pass, its most common use is as a means of finishing.

It is not a stroke of luck, however. It is the best course of action in certain situations, such as off of a chip pass near the goal, and can be premeditated and practiced. Because of its difficulty and "desperate" nature, it is not likely to draw criticism if it fails. Basically, you have nothing to lose with this kick.

Kicking a ball that is positioned over your head requires quick thought and action. It demands a high degree of agility, coordination and timing, along with a bit of courage.

Overhead kicks fall into two categories. One is a hooked volley taken over the shoulder. It is, in effect, an exaggerated version of a high volley. The other is a pure overhead in which the back is parallel to the ground and the kicking leg meets the ball near eye level or higher. These kicks are usually made in a sideways direction, although sometimes they can be made backward, and usually are made on the run.

Once viewed as a special tool for an elite group of gifted players, the overhead kick is becoming more traditional in today's advanced levels of play. One of the greater obstacles to learning it is overcoming the fear factor and learning how to land. It then becomes a matter of practicing it and learning when to apply it in games.

Practice activities

You can practice shots from difficult angles on the field or against a wall. If you do not have access to a goal, kick a ball at a target on a wall from sharp angles to simulate game situations. You can make the activity more efficient by having a partner receive your shots and kick them back to you against the wall. You can even have a goalkeeper play in front of an area marked off on the wall to simulate game action even more.

It is important to kick moving balls in your practice activities. Other than free kicks, it is extremely rare to have an opportunity to kick a still ball during a game, so make your practice as game-like as possible.

Volleys are somewhat difficult to practice, because each one you take in a game will be different. They are a result of timing and touch, which are acquired through overall experience. You can work on the body motion needed to make the shot, and practice the shot itself, but these only provide the framework for game situations.

When you do practice volley kicks, have a partner serve the ball to you from various angles. If necessary, have your partner throw the ball to ensure an accurate serve.

Those who practice the overhead kick should begin by doing it on a soft surface, such as spongy turf, sand or even a thin mattress. This inhibits your takeoff, but helps you learn how to land. Use your arms and hands to break your fall.

At first, practice with lobbed balls thrown at head height. If you kick with your right leg, thrust your left leg upward and your arms forward. Your left leg should be kicked as high as possible until just before you make contact with the ball, at which time you straighten the knee of your kicking leg and strike the ball with a quick slicing motion. Keep your eyes on the ball until after you hit it, then concentrate on breaking your fall.

5
Receiving

Receiving, or trapping, is the art of bringing the ball under control and setting yourself up to dribble, pass or shoot it. It is not one of the glamour skills, and is difficult to practice on your own, so many players are lacking in this area. It is essential to good soccer, however, as it precludes dribbling, passing and shooting.

Although it is often preferable to play the ball with a one-touch shot or pass, most of the time you will have to bring it under control first. The fewer touches it takes for you to bring the ball under control, the more effective you will be as an attacker. If you need several touches before you can make a positive move, you give the defense time to adjust.

Ball control revolves around touch, which is the purpose behind improving your juggling skills. You should be able to bring the ball under control with your chest, legs, feet and even your forehead.

Because this is a "passive" skill, it is particularly important to be relaxed. Feelings of tension or apprehension will show up in a herky-jerky movement that makes it more difficult for you to control the ball. The ability to relax, however, comes only through confidence, which only comes from diligent practice.

The key to receiving a ball, whether it's rolling, bouncing along the ground, or dropping from the air, is to keep your eyes on it. Move forward

Receiving tips

- Move into the ball's path if possible.
- Decide early which part of the body to use in controlling the ball.
- Maintain proper balance so you can adjust to the ball's flight.
- Face the ball as it is moving toward you whenever possible, placing the controlling surface squarely behind the line of flight.
- Be aware of your surroundings so you know what to do with the ball by the time you receive it.
- Relax the controlling surface before contact and withdraw it as the ball arrives.

toward the ball to receive it, and be ready to give slightly when you make contact to cushion the impact, guiding it in the direction you want it to go.

• • •

Foot receptions generally are the safest and easiest receptions. The foot offers a relatively high degree of control, and enables you to move with the ball more quickly because you don't have to wait for it to drop from your chest or thigh.

The harder passes are more easily controlled with the inside of the foot. You usually are facing sideways to the ball carrier anyway, so this technique demands less adjustment. It is crucial to get into a balanced position early enough to allow you to raise your controlling foot in time to receive the ball. You must be able to judge the speed and flight pattern of the ball. Remember to get behind the path of the ball so that you can at least block it.

Your ankle should be locked in an upward position, with the inside of the foot facing the ball. Your knee should be slightly bent as you "catch" the ball. Cradle the ball against the ground, shielding it from the defense with your body.

The instep can be used to "kill" a flighted ball. This is a difficult technique that requires exact positioning and rhythm, but you can then move with the ball quickly. The ball also is not likely to squirt away, which can easily happen on wet turf.

The outside of the foot is less common and less effective for stopping a ball, but has its place. It can be a surprise move that keeps an opponent off balance. The technique for this reception is much the same as with the inside of the foot, but with a different contact point. It can be used with a rolling ball or a falling one.

The sole of the foot can be used to stop rolling balls, but it is a dangerous method if defenders are applying pressure because the ball can easily squirt away. If the field is wet, you should be even more cautious.

The reception is executed by moving in front of the ball's path, lifting one leg, bending the knee, locking the ankle in an upward position and wedging the ball against the ground. Withdraw the foot upon contact to cushion the impact.

• • •

Thigh receptions add another important dimension to your game, although many passes that you can receive with the thigh also can be taken with other parts of the body, from the feet to the chest.

Catching the ball with the thigh enables you to move the ball more quickly to your feet. You also can disguise your intentions more easily than you can when you catch the ball with your chest. Most passes that you receive with your thigh, however, will be taken when you are not pressured by the defense, and when you are not expecting a pass.

The same basic receiving principles apply to the thigh as to the feet. Make your decision early if you can, although you don't have to give away your intention to the defense. Remain balanced and relaxed so that you can cushion the ball's landing. Know what you will do with the ball by the time you get it.

Lift your leading leg to make contact with the ball when your thigh is parallel to the ground, or slightly lower. Try to catch the ball on the upper thigh area, then withdraw it on impact with a short, sharp movement to deaden the ball. Your non-kicking foot should be in line with the pass, not sideways.

Although the thigh offers a larger area of cushion than the feet, you still need to keep your eye on the ball until after it drops. As you progress you can practice catching the ball on the move. You cannot force a thigh

reception, though. If the ball is not in the proper place to catch the ball with your thigh, use the foot or chest instead.

Unless you are equally adept with both feet, use your strong leg whenever possible. This gives you more control, and enables you to drop the ball to your strong foot more quickly. Ultimately, you will want to become equally skilled with both legs.

• • •

Chest receptions have become much more common in recent years. Once thought to be flashy or even a bit silly, they now are recognized as a very effective reception. The chest, after all, is the largest area of the body with which you can control the ball. Why not use it?

A chest reception enables you to change directions quickly, because your feet can move as you are catching the ball. It also is relatively safe; you are unlikely to lose possession off of it. Many chest receptions are made off of punted balls by the goalkeeper.

Your intention to make a chest reception is easily picked up by the opposition, so you must be quick to meet the ball rather than waiting for it to come to you. Otherwise, the pass might be intercepted. Balance and positioning are important. Keep your legs apart, either side by side or one in front of the other, and your knees slightly bent so that you provide a wide landing spot for the ball. Expand your chest as the ball nears. Watch the ball right into your body, then withdraw your chest upon impact as you bend your knees. After the controlling touch, the ball can be played with the thigh or the foot, or played off the ground.

Executing this reception on the move is much more difficult, as you have less control with your chest as you do your feet or legs. If you want to advance the ball in front of you, stiffen your chest upon impact to deflect the ball ahead of you, rather than trying to deaden the ball. You can quickly catch up to it and play it from there.

• • •

Forehead receptions are the rarest and most difficult receptions, but can be used with dropping balls or horizontal balls that are head high.

You should time your leap so that you meet the ball at the peak of your jump. You then absorb the ball and descend with it, after which you can play it off of your body or let it drop to the ground. It is important to keep your neck muscles relaxed so that you can provide a soft surface to deaden the ball.

Practice activities

A simple game of "pitch and catch" can improve your skills in all of these types of receptions. Stand about 10 yards away from a friend and pass the ball back and forth, catching it with the various legal body parts. Pass the ball on the ground and in the air for variety, building up to longer passes and more difficult catches.

You can stand on opposite sides of a volleyball net or similar obstacle to practice receptions of higher passes. This is particularly effective for chest and forehead receptions. Make it realistic, however, by playing the ball after receiving it and returning it after two touches. Use a defender if possible. As you progress, work on passing the ball to an intended target as a one-touch deflection.

You also can kick the ball against a wall and receive it yourself, employing the various receiving methods. Kick the ball harder as you improve, and move forward as you receive the ball.

Another effective game for developing passing and receiving techniques is to form a circle of five offensive players around two defensive players. The defenders pressure the ball as the passers move it around, employing various passing and receiving methods.

Forehead receptions can be practiced with a tether ball. Tie a rope around a ball, or to it, and tie the other end to a crossbar so that the ball hangs at a level even with your forehead. Push the ball forward with your forehead. As the ball swings back, jump to meet it with the forehead. Pull you head back upon impact. You also can practice by throwing the ball high into the air and jumping to receive it.

You can practice with a friend by throwing the ball high in the air to each other and receiving it with the forehead. After receiving the ball, execute a foot trap and then play the ball.

6

Heading

Hitting the ball with your head as a means of passing or shooting is a skill unique to soccer, and merits special discussion. The game is played on the ground for the most part, but heading has an important place in it. It is much more than a show-off tactic, or a skill exclusive to clearing attempts or shots on goal. Every player should possess this skill. Heading has become increasingly common as a passing technique in recent years as the game becomes faster and players become more athletic.

It has been estimated that nearly one-third of all goals come directly from headers. This makes it an obvious element of attacking play. And if attackers are attempting headers, defenders must do the same to try to win the ball.

Many young players are afraid to execute headers because of their natural fear of being hit in the head, both by the ball or another person. It should be practiced in sensible stages so that players can overcome their reluctance and improve gradually. You can start with a lighter weight ball if you want to build confidence.

The best place to make contact is at center of the forehead, just below the hairline. Follow the ball closely as it arrives, keeping your eyes open and your mouth closed. The entire body absorbs the force of the ball, but most

Heading tips

- Keep your eyes open and focused on the ball until making contact.
- Use the middle of the forehead when accuracy is essential.
- Throw the eyes and head at the ball; attack the ball.
- Make your decision to head the ball early so that the trunk and neck can be cocked.

of the initial shock is taken by the muscles of the neck. Do not draw the head in; extend the neck to meet the ball, keeping the muscles flexed.

Learn to jump first off one foot, then the other and then with both legs to reach the incoming ball. As you jump, keep your head and upper body tilted back, then snap forward as you meet the ball. Use your arms to help in the liftoff and to keep your balance, but concentrate on keeping your arms close to avoid fouls.

Practice heading on the run, redirecting the ball to either side of the field. A skilled header can make a powerful shot, clear the ball out of danger or make a quick pass.

On rare occasions, you can head the ball with your feet on the ground. If a line drive comes your way, you can redirect the ball with the forehead rather than jumping to hit the ball with your chest or attempting a bicycle kick.

Heading is a means of passing or shooting, a one-touch technique. Therefore you need to make sure you tense your neck muscles and propel the ball, rather than relax the neck muscles as you would to receive the ball. It is a positive, aggressive move. Hit the ball, don't let it hit you.

When heading as a defender, your primary responsibility is to get the ball out of the danger area. If you can deflect the ball to a teammate in an open area, great. Otherwise, concentrate on preventing the opposition from regaining possession near the goal. As a general rule, crossing passes should be returned to the direction from which they came, but at times it might be better to deflect the ball to the opposite side.

Practice activities

The simplest way to get used to heading the ball is to hold the ball with your arms extended at a 45-degree angle and bring it down to strike the middle of your forehead. Repeat the action to become accustomed to the feel and to gain confidence.

Later have a partner hold the ball aloft with both hands, and jump to head it downward. Your partner should not let go of the ball. The purpose of this activity is to concentrate on proper takeoff and heading technique.

You can practice with a friend by standing about 10 feet apart and throwing the ball underhanded to each other high enough to be headed. This gives time for the person executing the header to lean back and thrust his body into the ball. You also can practice diving headers and flick passes in this manner. Start with lighter weight balls if you want.

A wall also is useful for practicing heading skills. Start by throwing the ball into the air and heading the ball against the wall. Then throw the ball against the wall and head the rebound. Work up to heading the ball on the run, either by receiving services from a friend, or heading rebounds off of a wall.

7

Throw-ins

The throw-in is a relatively simple soccer skill. Perhaps that is why it often is neglected by coaches and players. Throw- ins, however, account for more than 70 percent of restarts in soccer games, and teams can expect to make up to 60 throw-ins during an average game. It obviously is important to execute them well.

At younger levels of play, the throw-in is neglected as a skill. At higher levels, it is neglected as a means of strategy. Many players tend to see throw-ins as an opportunity to catch a quick break, rather than an opportunity to set up a shot on goal. The throw-in should be taken seriously. Rather than merely put the ball into play, it should initiate a purposeful attack.

Grasp the ball with both hands, spreading your fingers comfortably apart, place the ball well behind your head and position your left foot about a stride in front of your right. If it feels more comfortable to place your right foot in front, or to keep your feet together, do so. If you have one foot in front of the other, keep your forward knee bent.

You generate power from the hips, lower back, thighs, arms and wrists. Lean back from the waist, then straighten up and whip the ball away. Rise up on your toes as the weight shifts and be sure to follow through. The rules

Throw-in tips

- Use both arms equally to provide force and accuracy.
- Keep your fingers spread comfortably apart, with the thumbs nearly touching.
- Bend backward from the waist, then whip your body forward. Follow through with the arms and wrists.
- Propel the ball upward at a 45-degree angle. Rise up on your toes as you follow through, but do not leave the ground.

state that you must use both hands equally, deliver the ball from over the head and keep part of each foot on the ground.

You can throw the ball from a standing position or from a running approach. The running approach will enable you to throw the ball a greater distance. You should only use as much speed as can be controlled. A small skip-step before releasing the ball can help generate more power, and help you adjust your last stride to avoid a foot fault. The heel of the forward foot should be planted first, and the ball thrown upward at a 45-degree angle from a release point slightly behind or directly over your head.

An effective throw-in uses many of the body's muscles. Weightlifting can help improve your performance, as can performing the skill with a heavier ball to increase resistance. You can isolate specific portions of the throw-in to emphasize improvement in that area — by throwing from a seated or kneeling position, for example.

Practice activities

Practice throwing until you become accurate, even over long distances. Throwing against a wall or into a net is a good way to develop the muscles necessary for the throw-in, as is throwing a heavier ball.

You can make a game out of practicing this skill by placing targets on the ground and aiming for them. Do it in competition with a friend and keep score. Increase the distance as you improve.

Defense

Defensive play is not the glamorous aspect of soccer, but it wins games. No player is complete without mastering basic defensive skills, and no team can win a championship without being at least as proficient defensively as it is offensively.

The most important principle of soccer, of course, is ball possession. The basic object of any defense, then, is to limit the amount of time the attacking team has the ball, the amount of space in which it can operate and its options with the ball. Whether a team plays a strict man-to-man marking system, a zone, or a combination of both, defense breaks down to the ability of each individual to contain his man. This involves mastering fundamentals as well as developing discipline, concentration and patience.

Many of our players at Indiana University have gone on to play in professional leagues and with the National and Olympic teams. A major reason for their success is their individual mastery of the principles of defense. Our players spend a great deal of time throughout the year developing and refining their defensive skills, and that can make the difference between being a complete player and merely a player with special offensive skills. The modern game demands that players be skilled with and without the ball. No longer can a team afford to "hide" a player defensively.

Marking

The role of the defender is to stop the attacker and ultimately win possession of the ball. Your chances of doing so can be improved by following these principles:

- Pressure the attacker.
- Deny the attacker time and space to operate.
- Force the attacker to a weaker angle.
- Delay the attacker's approach to the goal.

The most basic element of defense is assuming a proper stance, with good balance. The ability to move quickly in any direction from a more or less static position is critical to a defender's success and is rooted in the ability to keep the body's center of gravity low to the ground.

Any deviation from the correct stance slows your reaction time and gives the opponent a valuable first step. Being able to shift your weight quickly in any direction is fundamental to sound defense.

Establishing your position in relation to the ball must be automatic at any place on the field. Keep your head erect so you can size up the position of all the players in your immediate area of the field.

Marking tips

- Assume a slightly crouched stance, with knees bent and the upper torso leaning forward from the waist.
- Hold the arms, bent at the elbow, a few inches away from the thighs to help maintain balance, and keep the head steady.
- Place your feet about shoulder's width apart, with most of the weight on the balls of the feet.
- Keep the body relaxed, like a coiled spring, so you can react to any situation by moving in any direction.

When you are pressuring an attacker with the ball, your first responsibility is to close down the space in which your opponent has to maneuver. Patience is a virtue here, as you do not want to overcommit and take yourself out of position; your first obligation is to slow down the attacker.

Your own quickness should determine how close you play the ball. The closer the better, up to a distance of four or five feet. Your job is to apply pressure to direct the attacker away from the goal, thus forcing him to a bad angle for a shot or pass. Tight pressure forces the ballhandler to make negative or square passes and denies penetrating through passes.

If you engage the ballhandler in a straight-on manner, you are conceding him the option to move in either lateral direction. It is better to deny him one or the other direction by addressing the ball at a 45-degree angle. This way, you can shepherd the ballhandler away from a clear shot on goal and toward the touch line or a supporting defender.

As you move from side to side, shuffle your feet and avoid stepping one across the other. When retreating, use a backpedaling motion. It is all right to give ground or drop back with an attacker as long as you continually engage the ballhandler and maintain the proper 45-degree angle to the ball. If the attacker pushes the ball by you, it usually is best to turn through the shortest radius and attempt to position your body between the attacker and the ball without causing obstruction.

While playing defense, it is important to follow the movement of the ball while simultaneously keeping track of the player you are marking. This requires a certain amount of peripheral vision. You generally want to stay between the player you are marking and the goal. By diverting your attention too closely to the ball, you leave yourself open to a blind side move.

While marking your man away from the ball, you want to stay within striking distance so that you can be in position to contain him when he receives the ball, or perhaps intercept a pass toward him. The normal distance to keep from your man when he has the ball is about two yards, adjusting for differences in quickness.

When your player receives the ball, you must focus directly on the ball. Avoid falling for any foot or body feints your opponent might use. This is easier said than done, of course. Keep in mind that you can feint a tackle to gain the advantage.

• • •

The only time it is legal to intentionally initiate contact with an opponent is when using a shoulder charge to execute a tackle. The side of the upper arm and the shoulder are the only areas you can use, and contact must be made on approximately the same area of the opponent. The arms must be kept close to the body, and both players must have at least one foot on the ground. The defender must be playing the ball, not the dribbler.

The shoulder charge is used most often to try to gain an advantage while competing with the opponent for a loose ball. You also can do it to ride the opponent away from the play or move in for a tackle after catching up with him.

As with tackling, timing is more important than raw force. A well-timed and well-placed bump often will put the dribbler off-balance, allowing you to get to the ball. Dribblers should meet an anticipated shoulder charge by leaning toward the tackler and matching his force. The defender then has two choices: faking a charge and withdrawing it, hopefully causing the dribbler to stumble, or simply overpowering the dribbler with a more powerful shoulder charge.

Before making a charge, the tackler should match the rhythm of the ballhandler. The thrust into the ballhandler should be made from a bent outside leg with a strong pushoff. Should the attempt fail, the inner leg can restore balance. The most common reason for failure on a shoulder charge is poor timing, which results when the defender focuses more on the ball than the dribbler.

• • •

Many times a defender's best decision is not to tackle, but to delay the ballhandler's progress simply by being in the proper defensive position and exerting pressure on him. This enables your teammates to come into a support position, and perhaps force an errant pass. Again, by denying options to the attacker, you make his movements predictable and enhance your team's chances of regaining possession.

This form of defense incorporates techniques called *jockeying* and *shepherding*.

When jockeying, the defender attempts to stall the dribbler's progress by retreating with him, putting enough pressure on him to prevent him from operating with complete effeciency.

The defender should attempt to keep the dribbler off-balance by feinting tackles, then withdrawing. This cat-and-mouse strategy occasionally forces a turnover, particularly if the defender has made successful tackles earlier in the game. A faked tackle also can force a dribbler into a vulnerable position, from where the defender can execute a successful tackle.

Another aspect of jockeying is to try to force the dribbler to do something he does not feel comfortable doing. If you know his strengths and weaknesses, try to force him toward his weaknesses. Perhaps he is less confident dribbling toward his left. If you can force him in that direction, you have a better chance of making a tackle or forcing a turnover.

Regardless, the defender should be positioned at an angle that blocks the direct route to the goal. One foot should be placed slightly in front of the other so that you are less vulnerable to feints.

By shepherding, a defender tries to force the dribbler into a desired area, such as toward a touch line, away from a teammate the dribbler might want to pass to, or toward an area where the defender has more help. This is done by positioning.

• • •

The best method of *clearing the ball* after winning it from an opponent is to make an accurate pass to a teammate who is moving upfield and into attack position. If a pass is not available, initiate the attack with a determined dribble forward. Sometimes, when under extreme pressure by your opponents, you must deliver the ball quickly and accurately upfield and out of danger to gain time for your teammates to regroup. On these occasions you must choose from a variety of kicks that are appropriate for long clearances.

Other times, a simple header puts the ball out of play and delays the attack. When packed in heavy traffic in and around the goal area, clearances with the head must be directed up and away from the area and never down to where an opponent might run onto the ball and get off a shot. In any event, the clearance should be as high, wide and far as possible.

Even when under extreme pressure, a good defender should know where his teammates are so that he can direct his clearance to a place where it can lead to an opportunity to attack. You also can drop a pass backward to a supporting defender or your goalkeeper, and initiate the offense from there.

Practice activities

Unlike offensive skills, defense cannot be practiced alone except for perfecting the proper stance, footwork and turning techniques. Defense can be practiced in many ways with partners, however. You can work on your skills in one-on-one situations or in multiple-player settings. Three-on-three matchups are good because you gain experience in defending both on and off the ball.

A simple game for two players is to conduct faceoffs similar to those in lacrosse or hockey. The players can stand shoulder-to-shoulder with the ball between them. Upon a verbal command, they fight for the ball until one wins possession.

9

Tackling

A successful tackle is the ultimate defensive maneuver because it regains possession of the ball for your team. You should be careful about attempting tackles, however, because if you fail you might set up a scoring opportunity for the attacking team.

The key to good tackling is knowing when as well as how. Players should not commit to a tackle unless they are certain of gaining possession of the ball, although leeway can be granted to certain players in specific areas of the field. Forwards, for example, can be given more latitude when they are in their offensive third of the field, but generally players should not take themselves out of the play and contribute to the vulnerability of their teammates. When you miss a tackle your team is reduced to a 10-man unit until you get back in position — which might be too late to stop a shot on goal. It is not an exaggeration to say that one missed tackle can cost your team a match.

The ideal time to tackle, generally, is when an opponent has just received the ball and is trying to bring it under control. If he has already gained control of it, you must be more cautious. A "fools rush in" approach will place your team in jeopardy. Wait until the ballhandler makes a slight mistake, leaving himself vulnerable. Otherwise, try to steer him away from the danger zone.

Tackling tips

- Assume a low, balanced position, then make the thrust quickly and aggressively from a close position.
- Make the tackle as the opponent plays the ball, wedging it between his feet.
- Use the foot closest to the ball.
- Thrust the tackling leg through the center of the ball.

Remember, you do not have to win the ball to fulfill your role on defense. If you consistently contain the attacker, sealing off his passing angles and delaying his advance long enough for your teammates to set up and provide support, you have been effective. Eliminating options of the attacker makes any threat predictable and allows your supporting teammates the chance to anticipate.

Still, you will have many situations when you should attempt a tackle. Tackles come in many varieties, but the principles of each are the same. You should remain focused on the ball, stay low to the ground to maintain your balance and make your move quickly and aggressively.

Effective tackling carries with it an added psychological bonus. If you can win the ball from an attacker early in a match, he more than likely will remember that everytime he has the ball in your area. He might react by forcing a pass just to get rid of the ball, or by worrying so much about maintaining possession that he ceases to make aggressive moves with the ball.

Smaller players sometimes are reluctant to tackle, but lack of size really is not a disadvantage; at times, in fact, it can be an advantage. Make your move count. A half-hearted attempt probably will result in failure, and perhaps injury. A positive, aggressive move is more important than sheer bulk.

You also must be prepared to react quickly if you do win the ball. Avoid the temptation to rest for a moment, basking in your glory. The moment you achieve control of the ball usually presents your best opportunity to mount a meaningful offensive threat. Move away quickly, playing the ball forward if possible, and look for an open teammate. After you commit yourself to a tackle, quickness is the watchword. Be quick into the tackle, out of the tackle and after the tackle.

You also should be quick to react if you miss the tackle, which at times will be the case. If this happens, you must rejoin the defense as quickly as possible. There is no time to pout over failed tackles. You should either get back as quickly as possible to cover your man or pick up another opponent who was left open by a teammate covering your man. Furthermore, you cannot let a missed tackle or two discourage you from trying again at an opportune moment.

• • •

The most basic of all tackles is the *block tackle*. When making this tackle from the front, first measure the speed and movement of the ballhandler as he approaches. For example, if the attacker is dribbling with his right foot, you can anticipate that on *every* other touch the ball is momentarily free. That is the instant you must move.

You must get within tackling range of the ballhandler. Close down on your opponent, remaining composed and balanced. When an opening presents itself, thrust your right foot (or the foot closest to the ball) with the ankle locked into the path of the ball and shift your weight to stop the ball. Then follow through with determination. You need to maintain a low profile to keep your balance as you attempt to force your body between the opponent and the ball. You cannot just stick a leg out and hope to win the ball. Block tackling requires the force of the entire body.

Contact must be made forcefully through the middle of the ball. If possible, use the inside of your foot, as you would with a push pass. You also can use the sole of your foot in the same manner you have practiced as a trapping tool to capture the ball from an opponent.

If you fail to win the ball, and you have maintained good balance, you can thrust your other foot forward to make another attempt.

• • •

A *side block tackle* is more like stealing the ball. The fundamentals are the same as from the front, but the timing is more critical.

Move to a position as close as possible to the ballhandler. With your supporting leg slightly in front the ball, pivot into the opponent simultaneously with your shoulder and your tackling leg. You must be able to make contact with the ball with the outside of your tackling foot with enough force to halt its forward movement or flick it away.

Executing a *sliding tackle* in its various forms is difficult, and should be used only as a last resort. Like the slide in baseball, the sliding tackle is a way of falling while maintaining control. The defender can simply push the ball out of play with his outstretched leg, or with the inner leg bent under; the other leg is used to swing into the ball. In the hook-slide tackle, the outer leg is bent and the tackling leg extended to flick away the ball.

• • •

Rear tackles should be discouraged and attempted only by the most skilled players because of the risk of injury to yourself as well as the ballhandler. It is a desperate measure and should be used sparingly, if at all. You risk being charged with a tripping penalty and giving up a free kick, or being beaten so badly you will not be able to recover.

It is best to use the outside foot when making a sliding tackle; if the dribbler trips, it is more likely to be considered an accident. You also should approach the dribbler from a slight angle rather than directly behind the dribbler if possible.

The best time to go to the ground for the ball is when the attacker has a breakaway opportunity and you must make a desperate attempt to strip the ball away, or when the attacker is near the goal line or touch line and you can play the ball dead. As a last resort, a rear tackle might be appropriate when the attacker has a breakaway, but it is not likely to be appropriate near the goal line or touch line.

Practice activities

Tackles require a great deal of practice. You should learn to make them with both feet, from all angles.

Beginners should practice on soft ground, and perhaps while wearing long pants and pads to help overcome the fear factor. It is better to wear soft-soled shoes rather than soccer shoes to reduce friction and the chance of injury.

Start by practicing the tackling techniques against a still ball, with no opponent. Then work against a dribbler, increasing the pace as you progress.

⚽10
Goalkeeping

If you had to pick one position on a soccer team that is most important, it would have to be the goalkeeper. Simply put, when other players make a mistake, it doesn't lead directly to a goal. When the goalkeeper makes a mistake, it's a goal.

Because of his unique status, the goalkeeper can influence a game, positively or negatively, more than any other player. A poor play can ruin the hard work of 10 other players. A good play can cover up for someone else's mistake. The same applies to the psychological state of a team. A muffed save that allows a goal can drain the emotion from the entire team. A brilliant save that prevents a goal can lift everyone's spirits.

It is ironic, then, that goalkeepers are often neglected by fans, players and even coaches, as if they were some sub-category of soccer player. This is particularly true at younger levels, where coaches tend to pick their field players and then fill the goal with a less athletic kid because he won't have to run as much. If anything, it should be the opposite: the most athletic kid should be in goal.

You are not going to have a successful team without a good goalkeeper, and you can't win a championship with a merely average goalkeeper. No matter how good the rest of your defense might be, you aren't likely to keep

Goalkeeping tips

- Keep your feet shoulder width apart, with the weight forward on the balls of your feet. Your hands should be held slightly outside the line of the body and waist high, with the palms facing each other or toward the ball.
- Keep your eyes focused on the ball as it approaches the net. When the goal area becomes crowded, it's easy to become distracted and check on the position of teammates and opponents. The ball is the most important thing to worry about.
- Use both hands to catch the ball whenever possible. Two are better than one.
- Get your body behind the ball whenever possible, even for simple shots, so that if the ball slips through your hands your body will block it.
- Catch the ball rather than swatting it away whenever possible.

a good opponent from getting shots on goal. If your goalkeeper is mediocre or worse, some of those shots will get through.

A goalkeeper must have a unique combination of physical and emotional qualities. He needs the footwork, quickness, strength, eyesight, and judgement to stop shots on goal. He also must have courage, persistence, confidence, poise and leadership. He must watch the ball and the play, but at the same time keep an eye on the opponents and their defenders. He's the one pulling the strings; he's the director of the play.

It's no wonder, then, that great goalkeepers are a rare breed and that most of the great ones are relatively old. The job requires the kind of knowledge and maturity that can only be developed through experience.

You want a goalkeeper who's verbally active. That doesn't mean someone who just makes a lot of noise; they drive you crazy. You want someone who offers constructive communication and direction.

If you have a goalkeeper on the back line who's quiet and isn't saying much except "Get it out!", or "Don't let them shoot!" you've got a problem. That indicates a passive, fearful approach, which you can't have at that position. Your goalkeeper has to have the type of personality that wants to be challenged. He needs to be thinking, "Try to beat me!" You want that instead of "Get it out!"

Goalkeepers at the major college level are recruited by position. You can't convert one at that late stage very well because the job is too specialized. At younger levels, though, it's good to rotate the players in and out of the goal so they appreciate the skills and demands of the various positions. It's also a good way to find your leadership. A player who naturally takes charge in the goal is likely to be a good leader.

A great deal of time must be spent with the goalkeepers, and their training has to be specific to the position. We like to train in a functional setting and incorporate them into the exercises with the rest of the team, although they still need specific training before or after practice. They need to receive a lot of services of the different varieties. A lot of it is simply repetition training.

Goalkeepers must have good hands, good depth perception and judgement of the flight of the ball. They have to have cat-like reflexes and good footwork. Footwork is often neglected in training, but it is crucial. And of course they need power to dive. They have to do it all.

Goalkeepers are specialists, but they should be encouraged to take part in training with the rest of the players so they can appreciate the various skills and learn to use their feet. The rules now are more restrictive regarding the goalkeeper's use of the hands, so foot skills will continue to become more important.

Mentally, goalkeepers have got to be really tough. They can't let the pressure bother them. They've got to be able to handle that. They can't let a goal get them down.

Goalkeepers often are called masochists. They have to love pain because they have to be trained hard and get down in the mud and bounce their body off the ground. You've got to be able to take a charging player coming in and take a shot flush in the face without closing your eyes. You have to be fearless. It's not a position for anyone faint of heart.

Aside from the physical and emotional qualities, the great goaltenders also have an extra sense, that feel of being in the right place, of being lucky. Sometimes people will say a goaltender is lucky. More likely, he has a knack for being in the right place at the right time, almost a sixth sense. That is the skill of anticipation, which is largely developed through experience.

• • •

A common shot for the goalkeeper to stop is the rolling ball. The safest defense for these shots is to kneel, which provides three barriers — the hands, the legs and the upper body — for the ball to penetrate in reaching the goal.

A bouncing ball is more difficult to stop because it is unpredictable. This might call for an alteration in stance, such as keeping the knee off the ground. The most difficult bouncing shots to stop are those that bounce directly in front of the goalkeeper. If possible, the keeper should play the shot at the peak of its bounce.

The most basic save is the ball taken in the stomach or chest. Get your body behind these shots whenever possible and catch the ball with both hands. Your body should give a bit upon impact, just as it does when receiving a pass, so that the ball does not bounce off of it.

Shots arriving at head height and higher are more difficult to stop. They must be caught, or at least deflected, with the hands pointing upward. The fingers should be spread wide, and the thumbs should be nearly touching. Catch the ball if possible, bending your elbows to cushion the impact, rather than batting at it. After securing possession, cradle it to your body as quickly as possible.

When jumping to stop shots on goal, get a running jump and leap off of one leg whenever possible. You should bend the knee of the leading leg slightly for protection against opposing players. Do not bend both knees, however, as that makes it more difficult to maintain your position in the air and to land properly.

• • •

Crossing shots are even more difficult to contend with. Goalkeepers have more time to prepare for crossing shots, but they are more difficult to stop because of the less predictable line of path.

Successful goal defense starts with proper positioning. If the shooter is at the far flank, you should play near the far post. This provides you with a wider range of vision and gives you more time to play the ball. It also is much easier to defend a shot while moving forward than while moving backward. If the ballhandler moves in, then you must adjust your position.

Positioning is largely a matter of experience. As a general rule, the closer to the halfway line the cross is made from, the further you can afford to be out of your goal. Of course, the angle and speed of the cross also will influence your strategy.

You should be positive about leaving the goal for any balls, as a mistake could lead to obvious disaster. Goalkeepers cannot be indecisive or hesitant in these instances. If you are, you not only will have more difficulty playing the ball, you also leave your teammates in a confused state of mind.

• • •

The decision whether to catch or punch the ball also must be made quickly. You might have to change your mind at the last moment on occasion, but doing so increases the possibility that you will mishandle the ball.

On some occasions — such as when the goalkeeper cannot reach the ball well enough to make a clean catch, or when the goal area is too crowded with players and landing is difficult — it is best to punch the ball. Punching is similar to defensive heading. You want to achieve maximum height and distance so that you can clear the ball out of danger. If possible, hit the ball while on the run and strike it at the peak of your jump, like a volleyball player does when spiking it across the net. Strike the ball with the flat part of your fist between the knuckles and the lower joints of your fingers. Follow through for maximum power.

You then must recover quickly, so that you are in position to defend a quick followup shot.

• • •

Diving saves are the most glamorous for the goalkeeper, attracting the kind of attention and appreciation normally reserved for goal scorers. Goalkeepers should resist the temptation to show off, however, and dive only when absolutely necessary.

You risk embarrassing yourself, not to mention giving up a goal, if you dive for a ball too close to you. You might dive over the ball as it scoots underneath you into the goal. You normally need to dive only on short, hard shots that provide you with little reaction time. On longer shots, you should be able to pick up the flight of the ball early and move into a position to make a more routine save.

Part of the benefit to this approach is psychological. If you make your saves appear easy, if you can snatch a well-struck, well-placed ball out of the air with an air of nonchalance, you can frustrate the attackers or perhaps even break their spirit. Save your dives for when they are truly needed.

When a dive is required, it is important to keep your head up and eyes on the ball so you do not lose its flight pattern. Take a few small steps before taking off with a sideways skipping motion on the balls of your feet. Do not cross your legs when moving sideways. You might trip; at the very least your reaction time will be slowed. Jump off of the leg nearest the ball in a sideways motion so that you can remain focused on the ball. This final step, called the *power step,* provides the momentum for the dive. Keep your arms outstretched with your fingers spread. Your hands should absorb the impact rather than batting the ball back onto the playing field. Draw the ball into your body as quickly as possible.

Of course soccer is too fast-paced and unpredictable to be able to play the position by the book all the time. You will have occasions when you must rely on instinct, athletic ability and perhaps a bit of luck to stop a shot. Perhaps you'll be able to stick a leg out to deflect a shot like a hockey goalie, or you'll misjudge a ball but make the save anyway with a last-second adjustment.

The fundamentals, however, will see you through most jams.

• • •

The one-on-one situation against an attacking opponent offers the greatest challenge for the goalkeeper, and puts him in the spotlight for one brief, shining moment.

The crucial skill in these situations is to find the proper time and place to engage the attacker, limiting his options and angles to narrow the size of the target he has to shoot at. It is easier said than done, however.

If the goalkeeper advances too far, he leaves himself open for an easy chip shot into the goal. If he advances too soon, the attacker can pass off to a teammate, who will have an open shot. If he advances too quickly, failing to maintain balance, the attacker can beat him off the dribble for an uncontested shot on goal. If he doesn't advance far enough, the attacker has a large target area to shoot at.

The rule of thumb is to advance as fast as possible while the ball is outside the playing distance of your opponent, but to be more cautious if the attacker has control. If you can beat your opponent to the ball, you can avert the scoring threat before it has a chance to develop. Your best hope after the attacker has the ball is to force the attacker wide of the goal to reduce his shooting angle, and to buy time for defensive help. Feints can be effective in these situations to keep the attacker off-balance.

If you plan to try to tackle the ballhandler before he can get a shot off, you must make a positive, aggressive move for the ball. You'll only get one chance, and if you miss, the attacker will have a clear shot on goal. One approach is to wait for the dribbler to look at the ball and then go for it. Other goalkeepers prefer to watch the dribbler's feet and wait for an opening.

It is best to dive head first for the ball so that you can get your hands on it and maintain possession. You also will have the opportunity to make a last-ditch save with your feet if you are unable to control the ball with your hands. Dive sideways, to form the largest barrier possible, and protect your face with your trailing arm.

You risk being kicked in the head, but that's part of the job description for the goalkeeper. As I said, it isn't for the faint of heart. If you gain possession, clutch the ball to your stomach and wrap it up. At the very least, you should be able to deflect the ball away from the dribbler.

It is important to remember, however, that a relatively small number of the goalkeeper's touches during games come on actual saves. He is more likely to touch the ball on crossing passes or back passes from teammates.

• • •

A goalkeeper's job isn't done after he prevents a goal, however. The job is too demanding for that. If he gains possession, he has to concern himself with initiating the offensive attack for his teammates by throwing or kicking the ball. He is both the last line of defense and the first line of attack.

This requires that he possess a wide range of kicking and throwing skills, both for accuracy and distance. He assumes the role of sweeper at this point. At the moment the goalkeeper gains control of the ball, the opposing team is likely to be in poor defensive position. A quick punt or throw to the right place can lead to a quick scoring opportunity.

This is not to say the goalkeeper must get rid of the ball quickly. Often it is best to survey your options and wait a moment for something to develop. Both the goalkeeper and his teammates must be ready before restarting the play, regardless of the state of the defense.

Modern soccer has seen the throw become a more common means of distributing the ball than a kick because of the increased accuracy. This includes underarm and overhead throws, and anything in between.

Still, some occasions demand a kicked ball. Here, also, the goalkeeper has options, ranging from a drop-kick to a booming punt. The short kicks enhance accuracy. The long ones achieve distance, but are riskier. Drop kicks are most effective on windy days or for kicking into the wind. You should stress accuracy rather than distance with your kicks. Kick the ball only as far as you can be accurate. A booming 50-yarder does little good if it goes to the opponent.

Goalkeepers should spend a great deal of time practicing throws and kicks, as they are a vital part of the offensive attack.

Practice activities

Begin by receiving shots on goal from various distances and angles and at varying speeds. Practice on soft ground and wear protective clothing if you want, to help build the courage necessary for the position.

Work on engaging attackers as well. Start by having a friend approach the goal at a moderate speed, then dive to take the ball from him. Increase the pace of the drill as you advance. Later have him make a serious attempt at scoring.

By adding more partners, you can practice the timing of leaving the goal area for through passes, and work on short-sided games within a confined area. Ultimately, the goalkeeper should be involved in as many shooting drills as possible during practice, both for his benefit and that of his offensive teammates. Both sides should go all out to simulate game action.

You can practice throwing and kicking the ball against a wall, concentrating on form and accuracy. Later build up to throwing and kicking the ball to teammates at varying distances.

You can set up a simple three-man game to incorporate several goal-keeping skills. Have two teammates stand about 15 yards apart so that the three of you form a triangle. Begin by throwing the ball to one partner. He receives it and passes to the other partner, who fires a shot back at you. Increase the distance as you progress. If you like, the second partner can engage you one-on-one.

A more demanding exercise is to stand a few yards away from a wall with two partners further away from the wall. They alternately throw or kick the ball against the wall, from varying angles, and you play the rebound, either deflecting the ball or catching it. This simulates the fast action that occurs around the goal during games and sharpens the goalkeeper's reflexes.

Activities

The number of activities or games that can be utilized to improve your soccer skills is limited only by your imagination. Several basic and popular ones are included in this section, but do not hesitate to make up your own.

All practice activities should highlight the fundamental soccer skills: dribbling, passing, shooting, heading, receiving, goalkeeping and defense. The best ones involve several players and several skills. A group activity that focuses on passing, for example, also is likely to improve receiving skills. An activity that features shooting is likely to help goalkeepers.

Most of the activities included in this section require the use of a soccer field, or at least a portion of one. Soccer skills, however, can be practiced almost anywhere ample room is available. The important thing with activities such as these is to have fun while improving your skills.

KEY TO DIAGRAMS

O	Offensive Player
X	Field Player
D	Defensive Player
G	Goalkeeper
F	Feeder
C	Coach
△	Cone
⊛	Ball
- - - ->	Pass
——→	Run
~~>	Dribble
·····>	Shot

Cone Relay

Skill: Dribbling

Area: Any area

Players: 6 or more players

Equipment: 1 ball and 4 cones per team

Alignment: Teams of three players each line up 10 yards from a series of four cones placed in a straight line, five yards apart. The first player in each line has a ball.

Procedure: The first player dribbles around the first cone in his line and back to the starting line. Each team member takes a turn dribbling around the first cone. Each player follows the same procedure.

Simon Says

Skill: Dribbling

Area: Center circle

Players: 10-20 players

Equipment: 1 ball for each player

Alignment: Each player has a ball inside the center circle. The coach also is in the circle.

Procedure: Players, while dribbling continually, must react immediately to the coach's commands. For example, "Dribble with the outside of the right foot!" Or, "Change direction!" Or, "Go backward!" Although commands are given verbally, the players are to react only when the coach's hand, held in a fist over his head, opens up. This forces the players to keep their heads up as well as listen for the commands.

Players who make mistakes, react late or react when the hand is not opened are eliminated and must go outside the circle and juggle the ball while the others continue. The last player remaining in the circle wins.

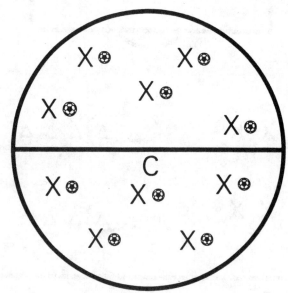

Tag the Dribbler

Skill: Dribbling

Area: Penalty area

Players: 5-20 players

Equipment: 1 ball per player

Alignment: Each player is in the penalty area with a ball.

Procedure: The game is played like tag, except each player is dribbling a ball. One player who is "it" chases the other players and tags anyone he can. He must maintain control of his ball while tagging. The tagged player becomes "it" and continues the game, but cannot tag the player who tagged him. A player is "it" if he loses control of the ball and it goes out of the penalty area. All players must continue moving even if they are not being chased. The coach or a bystander should call out the name of the player who is "it."

Variation: More than one player can be "it."

Circle War

Skill: Dribbling and shielding

Area: Center circle

Players: 2 or more players

Equipment: 1 ball per player

Alignment: Two teams of equal numbers stand in the center circle. Each player has a ball.

Procedure: On a signal, all players dribble within the center circle. While dribbling, the players on each team try to kick the balls controlled by players on the other team out of the circle. The team that kicks all the opponents' balls out wins.

Variation: Play individually. The last man in the circle with a ball wins.

Cone-y Island

Skill: Passing

Area: Center circle

Players: 12 players

Equipment: 6 balls and 16 cones.

Alignment: Two teams of six players each spread out around the center circle. Each player should have a partner directly opposite him, and each pair has one ball. Sixteen cones are placed anywhere in the circle.

Procedure: At a signal, the players start kicking the balls at the cones and continue kicking until all the cones are knocked down. The team knocking down the last cone wins.

Variations:

- Instep kicking only.
- Right or left foot only.

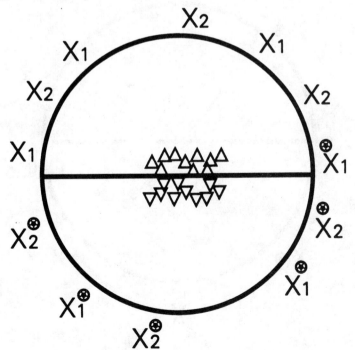

Dodge 'em

Skill: Passing

Area: Center circle

Players: 12 or more players

Equipment: 8 or more balls

Alignment: Eight players, each with a ball, spread around the center circle. Four players are within the circle.

Procedure: The outside players try to hit the middle target players by passing the ball with their feet. As a player is hit, he joins the outside group. See who lasts the longest. When all the target players have been hit, four new players get a chance to be in the target group.

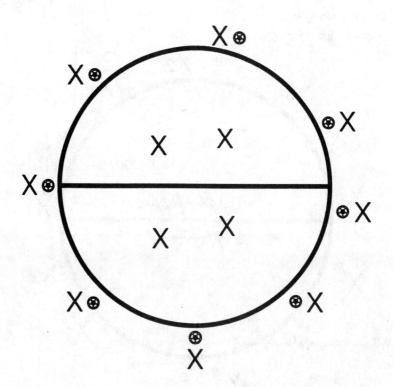

Ball Control

Skill: Passing and receiving

Area: 1/2 field

Players: 12 or more players

Equipment: 1 ball

Alignment: Two teams of six players each occupy one half of the soccer field. One team has the ball.

Procedure: The team in possession of the ball attempts to complete 10 consecutive passes against the defense. A new count starts whenever ball possession changes. The first team to complete 10 consecutive passes wins.

Keep it Alive

Skill: Passing and receiving

Area: Any area

Players: 8-12 players

Equipment: 1 ball

Alignment: Two lines of six or fewer players, about 10 yards apart, stand opposite and about 10 yards from two other lines of players. The first player in one line has a soccer ball.

Procedure: The player with the ball makes a ground pass to the first player in the line opposite him and goes to the end of that line. The player receiving the ball makes a one-touch pass to the first player in the diagonally opposite line and goes to the end of that line. This routine is repeated until an error (an errant pass) is made, after which the player making the mistake restarts the routine. Count the number of consecutive one-touch passes. Set a goal to reach or try to improve the best performance each time.

Shoot and Run

Skill: Passing and receiving

Area: Center circle

Players: 10-15 players

Equipment: 1-5 balls

Alignment: The players spread out around the center circle. One player has a soccer ball.

Procedure: The player with the ball passes to any other player and then sprints to that player's spot. The player receiving the ball continues the passing and sprinting action. Passes should be one- or two-touch. As skills permit, add more balls up to a maximum of five. The object of the game is to make as many consecutive passes as possible without an error, without any balls touching another ball or player, and without players running into each other.

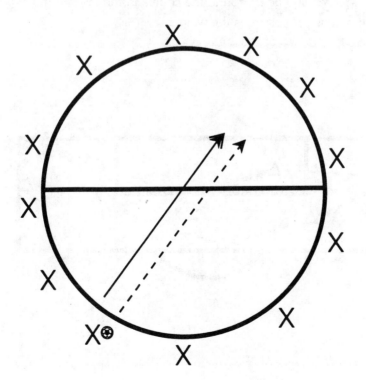

Fore!

Skill: Passing

Area: Penalty area

Players: 2 or more players

Equipment: 1 ball per player, 9-18 cones

Alignment: Each player has a ball and stands at a spot five yards from the first cone. Cones or markers are scattered throughout the area.

Procedure: Each player competes against a paired opponent to see how many passes it takes to travel completely around the course, using only inside-of-the-foot passes. Shots must touch or pass through the markers before players can move on to the next "hole." The players alternate passes. As in golf, the lowest score wins.

Variations:

- The player who goes around the course in the fastest time, regardless of the number of passes, is the winner.
- Increase the size of the area.

Triangle

Skill: Passing and receiving

Area: Any area

Players: 3 players

Equipment: 2 balls

Alignment: Two field players, each with a ball, face a third player so that the three form a triangle.

Procedure: Players X1 and X2 take turns serving balls to X3. X3 returns balls for one minute by head, instep volley, and instep half volley passes. The balls are then served to the chest of X3 who controls the balls to his feet and makes volley and half volley return passes. After X3 has practiced all the skills, the players switch places until each has received serves.

Turnabout

Skill: Passing and receiving

Area: 10 yd. by 10 yd. area

Players: 4 players

Equipment: 1 ball

Formation: X2 stands between X1 and X3. X4 stands beside X2 providing passive pressure.

Procedure: X1 passes to X2. The pass may be on the ground, or in the air to the thigh, chest or head. Upon receiving the ball, X2 turns in one smooth movement and passes to X3. While X2 is doing this, X4 may pressure, even bump, X2. After the pass to X3, X2 faces X3 and awaits a return pass. Upon receiving the return pass, X2 turns and passes to X1. The drill continues in this fashion for a prescribed period, usually one minute. After that time, players change positions.

Do or Die Baseball

Skill: Passing and receiving

Area: 1/2 field

Players: 10-40 players

Equipment: 1 ball and 3 cones

Formation: The players are divided into two teams of equal numbers. The team "at bat" is the offensive team and forms a line on the goal line outside the goal. The defensive team spreads out in half field. One defensive player, with a soccer ball, is on the penalty mark. Three cones are used as bases.

Procedure: The player with the ball kicks a rolling ball from the penalty mark to the goal line. The offensive player "at bat" kicks the ball into the field and attempts to touch all the bases and reach home (the goal line between the goals) before the players in the field get the ball into the goal. The field players must use soccer skills to get the ball home. Each play is a goal or an out and each player has a turn "at bat" before the teams change. The game can be played for any number of innings.

Pass or Play

Skill: Passing and receiving

Area: 30 yd. by 15 ft. area

Players: 3 players

Equipment: 1 ball and 1 cone

Formation: A cone serves as a goal. An offensive player and a defensive player stand near the cone. A feeder, with a soccer ball, stands about 30 yards from the players.

Procedure: The offensive player checks toward the defender, then turns and sprints toward the feeder, who passes to the offensive player at the second position. The defender stays with the offensive player and applies pressure. Defense should start off as passive and increase to total pressure. The offensive player, by communicating with the feeder, will decide to pass back to the feeder or turn and attack. Two points are scored by the offensive player when he makes a successful attack by dribbling the ball under control to the cone, and one point each time the defender thwarts an attack. The first player to score six points wins.

Kick-off

Skill: Shooting

Area: 30 yd. area in front of the goal

Players: 2 or more players

Equipment: 10 balls

Alignment: Players stand 30 yards in front of the goal.

Procedure: Each player kicks a moving ball at the goal from 30 yards. Each player has 10 attempts to accumulate a score. Five points are awarded for a ball that enters the goal on the fly, three points for a ball entering on one bounce and two points for a ball entering on two or more bounces. The player with the highest score wins.

Give and Go

Skill: Shooting and goalkeeping

Area: 20 yd. by 20 yd. area in front of the goal

Players: 4-24 players and goalkeeper

Equipment: 12 balls

Alignment: Field players form two lines at the outer corners of the penalty area. One line of players is supplied with balls. A goalkeeper is in the center of the goal.

Procedure: Player X1 passes diagonally across the penalty area to player X2. Player X1 then runs toward the goal, receives a return pass from X2 and shoots on goal. To limit the possibility of poor kicks, shooters are encouraged to use the inside of the foot. Players X1 and X2 go to the end of the opposite line after their turn.

Run it Down

Skill: Shooting and goalkeeping

Area: 1/2 field

Players: 16 players and 1 goalkeeper

Equipment: 12 balls and 1 goal

Alignment: A feeder stands 40 yards from the goal with a supply of balls. A line of offensive players is on one side of the feeder and a line of defensive players is on the other side. A goalkeeper is in goal.

Procedure: As the feeder passes the ball forward toward the 18-yard line, the first offensive player and the first defensive player sprint to the ball. The offensive player must get to the ball and shoot on goal before the ball enters the penalty area. The defensive player sprints to defend. The two players switch lines after playing the ball.

Variation: Play without defensive players to add emphasis to sprinting and shooting.

Volley-ball

Skill: Shooting and goalkeeping

Area: 25 yd. area in front of goal

Players: 2-12 players and 1 goalkeeper

Equipment: 12 balls

Alignment: Players form a straight line 25 yards in front of a goal. Each player holds a ball in his hands. A goalkeeper is in the goal.

Procedure: The first player in line runs from 25 yards out and drops the ball to the ground on the 18-yard line and takes a shot on the half-volley. Shooters retrieve the ball if they miss the goal.

Variation: Kick the ball before it touches the ground (full volley.)

Quick Draw

Skill: Shooting and goalkeeping

Area: 1/2 field

Players: 12 players and 1 goalkeeper

Equipment: 6 balls

Alignment: Offensive players line up at midfield alongside the feeder. Defensive players form a line at the side of the field 18 yards from the goal. Two of the defensive players serve as retrievers.

Procedure: The feeder passes the ball forward for the offensive player to dribble and shoot. At a given signal, the defender sprints to confront the offensive player. The object is for the offensive player to get a good shot on goal before being confronted by the defender.

Run and Shoot

Skill: Shooting and goalkeeping

Area: 1/4 field

Players: 12 players and 1 goalkeeper

Equipment: 12 balls and 1 goal.

Alignment: The players, each with a ball, form two equal lines about 30 yards from goal.

Procedure: The players at the front of each line alternately push the ball forward on the ground and sprint after it. The player shoots as soon as he reaches the ball without breaking stride, using whichever foot is appropriate. Avoid dribbling or setting up for the "best" foot. Shots should be taken from between 12 and 18 yards. Each player retrieves his own shot and, staying out of the shooting area, returns to the end of the opposite line.

Turn and Fire

Skill: Shooting and goalkeeping

Area: Penalty area

Players: 10 players and 1 goalkeeper

Equipment: 10 balls and 1 goal

Alignment: A feeder stands about 20 yards from the goal. An offensive player stands near the penalty spot. A defensive player marks the offensive player. A goalkeeper is in goal. Waiting defensive players serve as retrievers behind the goal. Waiting offensive players help the feeder by supplying balls.

Procedure: The feeder serves a ball to the offensive player who shoots on goal as soon as possible. After the shot is taken, the feeder serves another ball. The offensive player is under constant pressure provided by the defensive player. Each offensive player receives balls continuously for one minute.

Variations:

- Offensive player receives balls for one minute or until goal is scored.
- Add competitive element by keeping track of the number of goals scored in the designated time.
- Use two defensive players against one offensive player.
- Use two offensive players. The player receiving the ball from the feeder passes, one-touch, to his teammate who shoots on goal.

Second Chance

Skill: Shooting and goalkeeping

Area: Penalty area

Players: Several players and 1 goalkeeper

Equipment: 10 balls

Formation: Players form two lines approximately 10 yards from and facing a goal. A goalkeeper is in goal. A designated shooter stands between the two lines.

Procedure: The shooter aims shots to a spot within reach of the goal-keeper. Shots are taken hard so that the goalkeeper will have difficulty handling them. A second or two before each shot is taken the first player in each line sprints at the goalkeeper. The objective of the offensive players is to convert dropped balls into goals. Shots are taken rapidly so that players keep moving. The goalkeeper rolls cleanly played balls back to the feeder. Offensive players go to the end of the opposite line after each turn, and the feeder is switched periodically.

Firing Squad

Skill: Shooting and goalkeeping

Area: Center circle or similar size area

Players: Several players and 1 goalkeeper

Equipment: 1 ball

Formation: The players position themselves around the center circle. A goalkeeper is inside the circle.

Procedure: Players on the circle keep the ball moving by passing first time. At any time a player may shoot at the goalkeeper. The goalkeeper must move so that he constantly faces the ball, anticipating a shot. After fielding a shot, the goalkeeper returns the ball to one of the players around the circle.

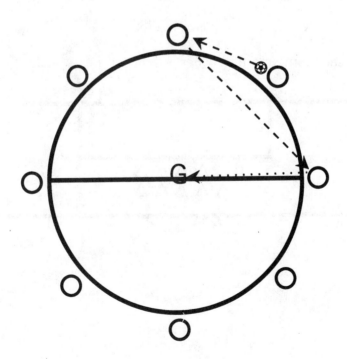

Ricochet

Skill: Goalkeeping

Area: Penalty area

Players: Feeder and goalkeeper

Equipment: Several balls and 12 cones

Formation: A goalkeeper is in the goal. Twelve cones are placed in front of the goalkeeper. A feeder with several balls stands at the penalty mark.

Procedure: The feeder shoots on goal through the cones. The goalkeeper attempts to save or deflect the balls after they bounce off the cones.

Run the Gauntlet

Skill: Offensive and defensive techniques

Area: 75 yd. by 15 yd. area

Players: 8-12 players

Equipment: 3 balls and 12 cones

Alignment: A rectangular area 75 yards by 15 yards is marked with cones. Cones are placed at 10-yard intervals within the 75-yard area. Offensive players line up at the entrance to the course. Defensive players position themselves between the width of the course at 20-yard intervals.

Procedure: An offensive player dribbles toward the first defensive player who advances from the first cone (20 yards from start) and attempts to tackle the ball. The offensive player attempts to beat the defensive player and, if successful, continues to advance to confront the next defensive player. The offensive player continues until he beats five defenders in order or until he loses possession of the ball. After the offensive player completes his turn he becomes a defensive player at cone five while all other defenders move up one cone. The defensive player who started at the first cone goes to the end of the waiting line of offensive players.

Hot Box

Skill: Offensive and defensive techniques

Area: Penalty area

Players: 12 players and 1 goalkeeper

Equipment: 8 balls

Alignment: Four attackers compete against four defenders and a goal-keeper in the penalty area. Two players, with a supply of balls, are located at the sides of the area, and serve as feeders. Two other players are outside the top of the area.

Procedure: One of the feeders crosses or passes a ball into the area, and the players compete against each other until a goal is scored or the ball is cleared out of the area. The players at the top of the area shoot or pass balls cleared their way back into the area. Otherwise, one of the feeders makes another cross or pass. All players are rotated after a specified period of time.

Variations:

- Change the number of players in the area.
- Use a strict man-to-man defense.
- Vary the types of crosses and passes.

Faceoff

Skill: Offensive and defensive techniques

Area: 1/2 field

Players: 12 or more players and 1 goalkeeper

Equipment: 3 balls and 1 goal

Alignment: Six defenders line up behind one post of the goal. Six or more offensive players line up at the center circle. A goalkeeper is in goal.

Procedure: A defensive player kicks the ball to the center circle. The waiting offensive player receives the ball and dribbles toward the goal. The defensive player who made the goalkick runs to meet the offensive player and attempts to tackle. If the defensive player is successful, the play ends and the offensive and defensive players go to the end of their respective lines. If the forward is able to maintain possession to the edge of the penalty area, the defensive player releases and the goalkeeper plays the forward one-on-one.

Head Game

Skill: Heading

Area: 60 yd. by 40 yd. area

Players: 6-9 players per team

Equipment: 1 ball and 2 goals

Alignment: Two teams equal in number spread out in the area. A player on one team has a soccer ball.

Procedure: The team in possession attacks and tries to score. The teams move up and down the field by players heading the ball to teammates. The ball may be caught and tossed for another header, or there can be continuous heading. The opponents can intercept the ball with their hands and start their attack. A ball touching the ground goes to the opponents. Goals are scored only by heading and play continues immediately.

Heading Over

Skill: Heading

Area: Center circle

Players: 14-22 players and 2 goalkeepers

Equipment: 1 ball

Alignment: One goalkeeper and several field players occupy each side of a center circle.

Procedure: The goalkeeper puts the ball in play by tossing it to the opposing side of the circle. Once put in play, the ball may touch the ground once on each side without penalty. The ball must cross the center line with a header, or a reaction rebound off a sharp header. Stress heading down. As in volleyball, you get three touches to a side, and no player may play the ball two times in a row. The first team to score 15 points wins.

Solleyball

Skill: Heading

Area: Volleyball court

Players: 6-12 players

Equipment: 1 ball and 1 volleyball net

Alignment: Two teams equal in number occupy respective sides of a volleyball court. One team has a ball.

Procedure: Play is begun by a head service from a front line player who throws the ball in the air and heads it over the net. The ball may be kept in play by using any legal part of the body, but the ball must be headed over the net. A game consists of 15 points. Points are scored only when serving. Teams rotate in a clockwise order when the serve is regained and a new player serves.

Part II:
Team Strategies

12

Coaching Philosophies

I was fortunate during my playing days to be associated with two great coaches, men who taught me many important lessons about soccer and about people.

Barney Hoffman, my coach at Myerstown (Pa.) High School, not only taught me the basic skills of the game, he also helped me develop a love for it, to appreciate it. While playing for him, I decided I wanted to coach someday, even though my parents wanted me to become a dentist. Mel Lorback, my coach at West Chester State College, was a master psychologist and a great motivator as well as a superb tactician.

I played on championship teams for both of them, teams representing small schools that overcame the odds and defeated much larger schools. From these two coaches, I "learned how to win." That's a cliche, but there's something to it. I suppose lessons can be learned from losing, but lessons can be learned from winning as well. Winners learn what must be done to win and develop the confidence needed to do what it takes in pressure situations. They develop an attitude that doesn't allow them to settle for anything but their best.

If an athlete grows accustomed to losing, it's easy for him to convince himself that winning really doesn't matter. It does. A victory isn't worth cheating for, but it's certainly worth devoting 100 percent of one's effort toward. When I recruit, I look for student athletes who share that attitude. Ability obviously is important, but I want someone who knows how to win and expects to win.

Of course it's impossible for everyone to come from a championship program. Everyone has to learn how to win somewhere, and that's a coach's primary responsibility: developing a winning atmosphere. That doesn't necessarily mean winning a championship every year. A program can be successful without ever winning a championship, if the game is approached with the proper diligence and attitude.

That's one of the things I've learned through coaching over the years. I wasn't a very good loser when I first started. I let the losses really get to me, and I was very hard on myself. I still wouldn't classify myself as a *good* loser, but I do cope with disappointment much better.

I've learned to focus on the effort and performance in a game rather than merely the score. Early on I sometimes lost sight of those values. I have coached many victories in which the performance level wasn't up to the standard that it needed to be. And I have coached some losses in which our effort and performance levels were quite good. As coaches and players mature, they have to realize that the score is not always a true indicator of performance.

● ● ●

Coaches approach their relationship with their players in different ways. Some make it a point to keep a distance, to create a more businesslike relationship. They don't believe they can maintain proper control over the team if they are too friendly with their players.

That works for some coaches, but a lot of the enjoyment of coaching for me comes from developing close relationships with the players. I want to have their respect, but I also want to be their friend. I don't feel comfortable having a barrier there. I want to be integrated with them; that's the atmosphere in which I feel most comfortable.

Coaches have a great opportunity to influence a young person's behavior. I spent 16 years in the classroom at Indiana University as a physical education teacher. I enjoyed the classroom, but I believe through coaching

I have a greater chance of influencing the young people with whom I come in contact. Coaching to me is a higher form of teaching. I can get to know each player and what makes him tick; get to know his girlfriend, his parents, his problems and so on.

Coaches have a wonderful opportunity to affect how young people think and how they act, even how successful they'll be in life beyond their college years. It's a tremendous responsibility. I feel I can have a more positive influence on my players and do a better job as a coach by being involved with them rather than keeping a distance.

Getting close to the players also helps me maintain a youthful outlook. It's enjoyable working with college students. It keeps me up to date on things — although I have to admit the music I have to listen to in the locker room isn't as enjoyable as it used to be. But I still like fooling around with the guys. I still arm wrestle with them, and I'm not afraid to joke with them.

Of course a coach's approach for the most part must depend on his personality and what works best for him. Some coaches aren't comfortable with informality, but it works for me. I believe players want to respond positively to the coach and please him. They should want to perform their best for themselves and their teammates, but the coach fits in there somewhere. If athletes are playing in spite of the coach, or playing *to* spite the coach — an "I'll show you" kind of thing — that can be counterproductive.

Coaches have to keep in mind, however, that they can't have positive vibrations with everyone. Some personalities just don't mesh. But that doesn't mean players they don't feel particularly close to can't be successful members of the team.

Coaches who take the approach I do have to be particularly careful to maintain proper discipline. A close relationship with the players doesn't have to mean letting them do whatever they want to do. We have policies for the team. They're printed out and given to the players and their parents. We don't have a lot of rules, but we expect them to be followed. They include the obvious things about drinking and drugs, treating their teammates and other students with respect, going to class, and so on. They're expected to use good judgement and common sense. And there will be times the coach has to put the hammer down and use discipline.

Coaches need to identify the players on their teams who display the proper leadership qualities, and then make sure that leadership is exercised. I believe a coach can do this more effectively if he spends casual time with his players. In a relaxed setting, he gets to know them better and see who among them is most admired. If a coach distances himself from the players, he isn't likely to learn who the real leaders are.

By allowing the leadership on a team to come forth naturally, a coach reduces many potential discipline problems. A coach can't keep everyone in line by himself — he's outnumbered, and he can't be with the players all of the time. Players are going to challenge the rules to see what they can get away with. Someone on the team must be willing to step forward and say, "Hey, if you screw up you have to answer to me," to teammates who might go too far. The players must take pride in the team by assuming responsibility for each other.

The most difficult discipline problem I've had at Indiana occurred when I had to release some players from the team. We were having poor leadership; the leaders were leading in the wrong direction. This happened during the spring, in the off-season. Finally the internal discipline came forward and the young players came to the coaches and said, "We don't like this, and we want you to know what's going on."

The coaches had sensed something was wrong, but we weren't completely aware of the situation. We might not have figured it out if some of the players hadn't felt comfortable enough to approach us with the problem. As a result, five players were suspended and three of them were not allowed to return to the team the following season.

It's a bit scary to drop good players like that, but in the long run it paid off. We missed the talent of the players who had been dropped, but as a result the team had better unity. If we had allowed those players to remain on the team strictly because of their talent, it could have proved disastrous, due to the fragmented nature of the team at that time.

We reached the No. 1 ranking in the country the next year, and went from an underachieving team to an overachieving team. The discipline and attitude of the players always carries over to the field. No matter how much talent a coach has, if the discipline and attitude are wrong, he and the team aren't likely to be successful.

If a coach doesn't have a close relationship with his players, he isn't likely to detect the team's possible internal problems. It frightens me to think what might have happened to the team if those younger players hadn't felt comfortable enough to come forward and talk about the poor leadership they were getting. If a coach makes it a point to distance himself from his players, he runs the risk of never being aware of the atmosphere among the team.

I've also had to suspend players from games over the years, although not very often. Perhaps a player didn't go to class, skipped study table, or didn't meet with his tutor. In a college program, academics must be the top priority. The players must realize their first obligation is to their education.

The emphasis on academics should occur at every college, as well as at younger levels. Even on youth teams, the coach should take an interest in the players' academic progress. Soccer, and any sport, can be a great means of motivating players in the classroom. If a kid knows that he's likely to have to sit out a game or two, or perhaps lose his place on the team if he doesn't put forth an honest effort in the classroom, he'll probably take a more serious interest in his academics.

• • •

One of the primary strategic decisions a coach must make is what "formation" to employ. Over the years, a dizzying variety of systems have been used — 4-2-4, 4-3-3, 4-4-2, 3-5-2 . . . you name it, it's probably been tried.

When I played in high school and college, and when I began coaching, the W-M formation was the most common system of play. Coaches tend to use what was successful when they played, and that was what most teams were playing at the time.

Today it is common to have three or four players in the back, with a deep sweeper or an advanced one. Most teams have two primary markers, maybe a third if the other team has a third forward. We're also seeing more players in midfield now, providing width to the offense. In attack, teams can play with one, two or three front runners, each with a specific role.

I'm not much for numbers, however. The fact is, the formation isn't nearly as important as the roles that are assigned to the players. When someone asks me what system I use, I just smile. From one year to the next it could be completely different. It also can be different from one game to the next, depending on the opponent and on our personnel.

Early in my coaching career we tried some things that were uncommon at the time, such as playing four in the midfield. In those days, before the program had become established, we had to make a lot of adjustments because we had such a diverse range of talent within the team. We had some players whose skills were excellent, as well as inexperienced players with technical and tactical deficiencies. This is bound to be the case for many teams below the major college level.

Having such varied talent forced me to be creative in determining roles that enabled the players to become more successful individually and helped the team become more successful as a unit. We played a variety of systems from year to year, depending on our individual talent, how we wanted to use our better players and how we wanted to hide the players who were just learning the game. That was a great training ground for me as a coach.

For example, I had one player, Karl Schmidt, who was an all-American in 1967. He would be a striker one game, the sweeper the next game and play in the midfield in the next. It all depended on our opponent.

I believe determining roles for the players is crucial to successful coaching. There are no secrets with the X's and the O's in soccer. We all know the same principles of play. What is most important is finding the proper blend for the talent.

Ultimately, the proper blend is to have an entire team of players who can play anywhere on the field, players who — aside from the goalkeeper — are completely interchangeable. Such a system places few restrictions on the players; it's free-flowing and somewhat ad- libbed, and places constant pressure on the defense. As a result, it's the most difficult to defend.

Holland, with its "Clockwork Orange" attack in the 1970s, came closer than anyone to mastering this approach. A few of our teams came reasonably close, such as the one in the early 1980s that won two national championships. We really confused and frustrated defenses who were accustomed to seeing players in the same positions on the field throughout the game.

However, an offense must have purpose. The players can't be running helter-skelter around the field, moving just for the sake of moving. The primary factor in deciding how a team plays, both offensively and defensively, should be determined by the capabilities of the personnel.

A coach obviously wouldn't ask a player who's a good defender but has poor attacking skills to go forward with the ball very often. A coach must determine the capabilities of his players and ask them to play within them. Sometimes coaches expect players to do things that they aren't capable of doing. To ask players to do things they have trouble doing not only hinders their performance, it can be psychologically damaging for them and for their teammates.

For example, in 1991 we had five or six freshmen who played a great deal. We had a difficult time early in the season determining where they fit best. We kept things simple early on. We used the KISS principle — "keep it simple, stupid." We were quite predictable for our opponents, but at least we weren't confusing ourselves. We started out the season playing with three front runners, three in midfield and four in the back with a deep sweeper.

As our players developed and we learned more about what they could do, we changed our system of play. We used one advanced striker, a forward who played underneath the striker, an advanced central midfielder, a defensive central midfielder and two players who played wide at midfield.

The way we played in our first game was completely different than how we played in the finals of the NCAA tournament. That was an unusual year because we had so many young players, but coaches must be flexible at all times. It's often a mistake to lock into a formation at the start of the year and stick with it.

Coaches of more experienced teams usually can afford to be more consistent in their approach, although they still should be willing to make changes if it improves the team. Players might improve, or possibly take a step backward during the season, and a coach should make changes to accommodate the fluctuations in performance.

I don't recommend that coaches adopt a system and say, "This year I'm going to play a 3-5-2." Some people today, for example, say, "You've got to play five in the midfield, that's the modern game." But there's no magic in the numbers. A formation does not win a championship, players do.

The successful coaches are those who are able to mold their players into a cohesive unit by figuring out how they best complement each other. If five different coaches could take the same 11 players and work with them in setting up a team, the one who could achieve the best chemistry — such as by identifying the leaders and workhorses, hiding the weaker players and taking full advantage of each individual's skills — would be the most successful. That's where a coach's sixth sense is important.

I always admired Harry Keough, the coach at St. Louis University, during my early years of coaching. I felt he had that knack of being able to put 11 players on the field and get the best out of them as individuals and as a team. I've also seen coaches who made me wonder, with all the talent they had, why they didn't have a better team. Perhaps they were too hung up on a system. That's a common mistake for many young coaches.

Sometimes a coach is influenced too much by another coach. He might think, "Indiana won the championship with this formation," or "St. Louis did it that way, so if we can learn how to play that system . . . " yet he might not even have players who can play that style.

I've seen coaches insist on playing counterattack, fast-break soccer, for example, when they didn't have the speed up front to beat the opponent's defense. That approach is suicidal without superior speed. I've also seen coaches who insist on slowing the tempo by trying to build an attack through short passing combination play, but they don't have players with the ball-handling ability or the intelligence to create. They might be better off playing with fewer touches and trying to penetrate more quickly — not just kick and run, but use fewer passes to advance the ball.

The system must suit the players. The talent on hand and the opponent's tendencies should determine the approach a coach uses for the next game. If the opponent is weak defensively on the left side, a team can concentrate its attack on the right. If an opponent gives a team room at midfield, it should be able to play to the players' feet at midfield and do more combining. If the opponent plays a pressurizing zone defense, a team needs to be able to change the point of attack quickly by playing with fewer touches. Teams must be flexible enough to make adjustments according to the strategy of the opponent.

However, this does not necessarily apply to youth teams. Coaches tend to want to over-coach younger players and make it too complicated. The game itself is a great teacher. It's fun by its nature, and coaches of young players should not get too caught up in systems and formations. Coaches should place them in an area of the field and give them responsibilities, but at the same time not stifle their creativity.

Young players should be allowed to show creativity and express themselves within the game. I hate to hear a coach yelling, "Get back there, what are you doing dribbling like that?!" That's part of the joy of playing. The beehive approach kids take, running after the ball in clusters, is only natural because they want to be in the action. To tell a kid to stand back and play only when the ball is in his or her part of the field takes the fun out of the game and doesn't teach him or her much.

Youth coaches still can teach basic principles of play both offensively and defensively, but they should regognize stages of development. The beginning players shouldn't be burdened too much with strategies and roles and formations. They should simply be allowed to play.

• • •

Coaches should not overlook the basic nature of their players in determining how and where they best fit into the team. Different roles favor different personalities. A primary attacker generally has a different personality than a strong defender, for example, and to place a player in a role poorly suited for him can cause problems.

Not every position has a personality profile, but on advanced teams it is important to find at least one player who has a nose for the goal — someone who has a great hunger to score. I've had players up front who were excellent ballhandlers, who could beat people and unbalance defenses and create good scoring opportunities, but then would find a way *not* to score. In the final analysis, nothing happened.

However, a less skilled player who doesn't have the same flair to beat the defense might be able to make something happen on the occasions when he gets into scoring position because of his confidence and the sheer force of his will. Coaches should look for that personality in at least one player. If they can find more than one player with a scorer's mentality, it's a bonus.

Teams also need players on the flank who have the speed to burn a defense and the ability and willingness to serve balls to teammates. We've had players who didn't have great speed but had great one-on-one moves, and they took more satisfaction out of an assist than a shot. Coaches should try to find that kind of combination, one in which they have primary feeders and primary goal scorers working together.

Coaches should continually be searching for a blend of players who can do different things. If they have too many in the same area who like to do the same things and have the same personalities, the combination isn't likely to work very well. Coaches might have two gifted scorers they want playing in the same area of the field, but the result is like a magnet: the like poles repel each other rather than attract. Both players might be extremely talented, but that doesn't necessarily mean they can play well together.

A coach, for example, might think he wants his best ballhandlers to play together at midfield; however, it might be better to move one of them to an attacking position and bring in a player who complements the other ballhandler. The player brought in might not be as skilled, but perhaps he'll be the ball winner who helps set things up for the scorer. Establishing the right blend, the right chemistry, is crucial.

In the back, coaches should look for players who are stable, dependable and competitive — players who want to establish authority and dominate the opposing attackers. Hopefully, at least one of them is also able to bring the ball out of the back and distribute it to initiate the attack. This can be a sweeper or another back player.

However, some players don't have the personality traits necessary to excel defensively. They're creative free spirits who want to be closer to the opponent's goal, where improvisation is a virtue.

Teams also need players willing to do the dirty work, such as running down loose balls, winning the 50/50 balls and stopping opponents. These are the elements coaches must sort out. An individual's personality has a great deal to do with what role he should play for the team.

My 1991 team exemplified the importance of developing proper chemistry. After struggling early in the season to get our combinations working, we moved a player up front who had never played a forward position; he had always been a midfielder or a defender. He was less gifted than the player he replaced, but his presence up front made the team more effective. He brought a fight and a spirit to the attack that lifted the other players. He didn't have the same flair with the ball as the other players, but his work ethic was infectious.

Because of our interchangeable approach, we generally don't recruit by position, except in the case of goaltenders. It often takes quite awhile to determine the position for which a player is best suited. Many of our excellent defenders were forwards in high school, for example. We try to find the best total soccer players, bring them in and teach them our system and our principles of play, and see what fits their personalities.

The coach's association with his players also comes into play here. If he has established a comfortable rapport with them, he can more accurately detect their personality traits and determine where they can contribute most on the field.

I also believe each team has an overall personality, and that should be considered in choosing its particular style. Of my three NCAA championship teams, the 1988 team had a different personality than the first two. It was more of a blue collar team. The players worked hard for each other, and didn't necessarily win by having more skill than their opponents. We had some great individual talent on that team, but not as much as the other two championship teams.

My championship teams in 1982 and '83, and the one that was runner-up in '84, relied more on raw talent. It seemed as though the best thing that could happen to them was for their opponent to score a goal early in the game; it was almost like they needed a wake-up call. They had a tremendous amount of confidence in each other and it showed on the field. They intimidated their opponents and wore them down mentally. The '88 team, on the other hand, simply outworked its opponents and wore them down physically. They kept coming and kept coming and never gave up. They seemed stronger toward the end of the games, and won a lot of games in the closing minutes.

• • •

The NCAA recently passed a rule limiting practice for Division I programs to 20 hours per week during the season. Some coaches aren't pleased with the cutbacks, but the NCAA might have done them a favor.

Longer is not necessarily better when it comes to practice. When I was starting out, I thought if I wasn't out there at least two hours or more I wasn't a good coach. But I've come to realize over the years that a practice does not need to last longer than 90 minutes if it is well-organized.

Our practices now are more streamlined, and they are better as a result. The players stay fresher throughout the season. They also are more enthusiastic about what they're doing when they know the practice won't drag on forever. Coaches at all levels should realize they can get their work done in a relatively short amount of time if they are properly organized. Keep the practices short and sweet whenever possible.

Coaches also should be flexible with their practice schedules. The best-laid plans on paper don't always work out well on the field. Sometimes coaches think they're being unorganized if they deviate from their schedule, but I consider that to be flexible and creative. A coach has to be able to adjust to his team's needs. Why emphasize ball control one day because the schedule he drew up several weeks ago says to, when recent games have made it clear the team needs to work on finishing or defense? A common sense approach works best.

As a young coach, I would outline a practice that included everything I wanted to cover. Then, even if the players struggled with something after we got on the field, I would stubbornly stick with the schedule. Sometimes a coach just has to scrap his plan and go on. I still map out our practice sessions, but I make it a point to remain flexible. It's not cast in stone by any means.

A coach must have a feel for the team. At times the players become psychologically stale; a coach must recognize this and make changes accordingly. Coaches cannot expect players to perform the same drills over and over again without losing interest after awhile. They must show variety and creativity in coming up with new activities and challenges so that practice is not too boring. At the same time, however, they cannot let a session become a circus. The trick is to find a balance between being well-organized and creative.

We try to take full advantage of the time before the official start of practice. Say, for example, most of the players arrive on the field, dressed and taped, at 3 o'clock, with the first formal activity not scheduled until 3:30. Each player, after proper warmup, should have an assigned activity to concentrate on during that pre-practice period to help improve his weaknesses. Too often players want to work only on their strengths when they are on their own. In excess, this amounts to little more than showing off. Coaches should make sure they are working to improve their weaknesses as well.

Many of the pre-practice activities can be done in small groups. For example, a player who is exceptionally strong at heading can work with teammates who are weak in that area. This is a free period, but should be organized sufficiently so that the players know what they must work on, and can do so without a coach directing them.

At 3:30, we would begin the formal practice by stretching as a group. Stretching is vital to the prevention of injuries and developing flexibility, therefore we treat this time seriously and use a full regimen of exercises.

This warmup phase can be completed with an activity that demands moderate movement. It should be an enjoyable activity that helps bring the warmup to a climax and encompasses various elements of the game. Playing five-on-two with a one- or two-touch restriction is a good activity for this purpose.

The next phase, which lasts 15-20 minutes, is devoted to the technical emphasis of the day, which would be a specific skill. We set up two or three stations, with a coach or player in charge at each one. If the emphasis for the day is heading, one station might concentrate on defensive heading, clearing the ball out high and wide. Another station could include services to the near or far post for heading on the goal. Each player, depending on his position or role for the team, should spend the appropriate amount of time at each station.

The next phase of training can be devoted to small group work and principles of play. This generally involves breaking the game down to its essential element — one-on-one offensive and defensive principles — so a great deal of time should be spent on activities that match one player against another. Use full-sized goals manned with keepers whenever possible, and try to incorporate a finish on goal with as many activities as possible.

We like to build up to two-on-three, three-on-two, three-on-four and four-on-three activities during this phase, and then continue building to larger groups — perhaps even a full-sided scrimmage. The game itself is a great teacher. It also is beneficial to impose conditions on individual players, or the entire team during the scrimmages to enhance learning, such as one- or two-touch restrictions.

If John is holding on to the ball too long during games, for example, we would impose the restriction that he must play one- or two-touch during the scrimmage. If Charlie is playing hot potato with the ball, we would require that he beat a man before he delivers a pass or shot. Defenders can be required to build up out of the back or bypass midfield.

Small-sided games, such as six-on-six, can be used in a confined area to concentrate on possession and combination play. Again, conditions can be set, such as allowing shots on goal only after a certain number of consecutive passes or touches.

Shadow play, in which the offense is set up to play against a limited number of defenders, can also be effective. The numbers can be increased progressively. The offense, for example, can work five-on-six or six-on-five, with the back four and one or two midfielders working against the attacking six. This can be done in a half-field situation with a particular mode of attack, such as having the front players work to create space for a midfielder coming through. Or, the midfielders can carry the ball into attack with the defense adjusting accordingly.

The point here is that scrimmages — short-sided or full-sided — aren't just games, they are opportunities to develop a tactical plan.

Restarts — free kicks, corner kicks and throw-ins — can be worked on during the pre-practice phase, and then later be incorporated into the more functional group activities.

Although I prefer to incorporate conditioning into the various phases of our practices, some coaches set aside specific time for it. If so, I believe it should be reserved for the final part of practice, therefore the players are fresh mentally and physically while practicing techniques and principles at the early stages of the practice session. Speed work can be scattered throughout the practice, but heavy fitness training should be done at the end of the session.

Coaches differ in regard to how much time players should spend scrimmaging. I'm an advocate of scrimmaging. The players are out there because they love to play the game. They've been playing it most of their lives and they enjoy it. Sometimes coaches get carried away with their practice plans. They forget why the players are there and what their primary objective is, which is to have fun and play the game.

That's one thing I've learned, and try to keep in mind at all times. Practice can't become a circus; it can't just be "fun day" everyday. But I work hard at trying to make sure the players enjoy it. And the one activity they enjoy the most is playing the game. Ask players what they want to do and they'll say, "Let's scrimmage!" They want to play, so we let them play. But we teach within the scrimmages.

Some coaches believe it's a waste of time to conduct full scrimmages. They don't believe they get any teaching accomplished, that they lose control. I disagree. I believe the game is the best teacher. Players can best rehearse tactics, establish tempo of play and work on combination play through scrimmages. It's one thing to look good in two-on-two situations or small group practice, but that doesn't always carry over to games.

Generally, our most recent game indicates what we need to work on during practice. We'll use video tapes to learn more about our strengths and weaknesses, and to check our statistics. If we are turning the ball over too much, we'll work on improving ball control. We'll set up activities that are relevant to our needs at the time.

• • •

The psychological aspects of coaching any sport are a real challenge. A coach wants to discover the key to each individual. How can he open that kid up? How does he get to him? With some kids it's a pat on the back, with others it's a stern hand. A coach needs to gain his athletes' trust so they'll work hard for him.

To do that, a coach must react to the players individually. He can't treat everyone the same. He must have the same rules and policies for everyone, but he has to adjust to individual personalities. Finding the best means of motivating each individual is a real key to building a successful team. A coach can have the greatest talent in the world, but if he can't reach the players — if he can't keep them motivated — he won't be successful.

One important method of motivation is to keep the practices competitive. We try to set things up so that our practices are more difficult than our games, and we make it clear to the players that positions can be won and lost in practice. If players start thinking they have their spot secure and don't have to work hard in training, then the coach has problems.

I like for a player to know that if he lets down there's somebody right there on his heels ready to take over. When that situation is established, a coach finds he doesn't have many players missing training; the injuries don't seem to occur as frequently, especially the psychological ones. Also, the overall effort put forth in practice is stronger. If the coach can keep the competition keen within his own team, it strengthens the team in many ways, both physically and psychologically.

The coach must also work to create an environment that helps the athletes develop confidence. He can do this in the way he conducts the practice sessions, and how he structures the team. However, as in the case of leadership, each team needs one or two team members who raise the confidence level of everyone. The coach can orchestrate it to a degree, but it has to come from within. It's like a symphony in some respects. The coach can provide direction, but the players have to want to perform.

Before a game, I'll talk about what we need to do, and perhaps about the importance of a game. I've also brought in guests, such as Coach Knight, to talk to my players — someone to add variety and give them something new to think about.

I used to give rah-rah talks in my early coaching years, but I've come to realize that the higher-level players have their own way of getting ready for the game. A couple of them might sit quietly in the corner, while others might be pumping each other up. A coach should allow for individual differences. Of course there might be some who need a spark, and a coach has to be able to provide that for them.

Overall, though, I'm not a cheerleader. I don't have my players running through walls to get to the field. That just doesn't fit me. They'd laugh at me if I tried it. But I do get intense. I love to compete, and that rubs off on the players. One of my teams in the early years gave me a plaque that read, "To Coach Yeagley, who has a burning desire to achieve." I believe that most teams reflect the personality of their head coach; the coach sets the mood. Yet all coaches must recognize the need to operate within their personality. If they don't, they'll wind up looking foolish.

The coach should also establish a sportsmanlike atmosphere. This should go without saying, but there are teams at every level, from youth leagues to professionals, that lack basic sportsmanship. Everyone wants to win, of course, but they should want to do it within the rules and do it with class. This is particularly important in youth leagues. It's disheartening to see coaches at that level screaming at their players, the opponent or at the officials. At that level more than any other, the coaches should focus on instilling sportsmanship.

The attitude toward the opponent, the officials and the game has to remain a positive one. It's ridiculous to try to find ways of getting around the rules or to try to physically eliminate an opponent. Coaches and players all have moments when they are reminded of soccer's overall place in the world. They should keep this in mind at all times.

• • •

If a coach is fortunate enough to enjoy continued success, he is faced with a new problem: complacency. As far as problems go, this is a good one to have, because it means he's accomplished something. But he must find ways to deal with it, both from within himself and his players.

A team is bound to have valleys of fatigue during a season, whether it is winning or not. Players get psychologically stale, and the coach must look out for that. Over the years the signs become apparent. The players might be arguing among themselves and appear to be losing their enthusiasm. They get grouchy. There are all kinds of tell-tale signs.

A coach can deal with this in one of two ways. He can crack the whip, or he can do something to break the monotony and give the players a new outlook. My approach in the early years was to bear down on the players even harder. We'd train longer and work harder when I thought the players were losing some of their intensity. Now I often go the other way. I might

give them a day off, or I'll have them do something like play soccer volleyball; something not directly related to the game, but something different and fun. If it's a wet day, we might practice dive headers and slide tackles in the mud. Or we might make the practices shorter.

At times such as these, a coach needs to throw away the plan for the moment and realize he's got a more important problem: getting his team back on track. A lot of times changing the environment and changing the activities does the trick. This comes from experience. It's a feel a coach acquires, and he has to know when to trust his judgement.

I've even done this before some very important games. The assistants might say, "We've got a huge game coming up and you want to cut practice to 45 minutes? We need to be working harder." But at a late point in the season the players can't be taught much of anything new. They aren't likely to improve a great deal with an extra hour of work at that point. They need to be refreshed mentally. It's a gamble, but with experience a coach develops a feel for his team's moods.

We start practice in mid-August and go two times a day. I can almost guarantee that by mid-September we'll have a stale period, and then two-thirds of the way through the season we'll have another one, and then at tournament time we'll have another one. People might think when a team is preparing for the tournament it should be getting psyched up, but it might be better to take some time off to get refreshed.

• • •

Soccer is a player's game. The coaching must be done during the week; after that the games are in the players' hands. In international competition coaches aren't even allowed to actively coach on the sidelines. We're allowed to do more in college, but many times the yelling, the *attempted* coaching, does more harm than good because the players have trouble focusing on the game.

A coach can substitute and make minor adjustments at halftime, but for the most part he turns the game over to his players and hopes they're prepared for all the situations they might encounter during a game.

This brings up the subject of "big games," which all coaches face. For a youth league coach, a big game might be one against the team that leads the division, or against the crosstown rival. Whatever a team's level, it will play some games that are more important than others, for various reasons.

The approach for games such as these should not change drastically. We lost in the final game of the NCAA tournament in 1976, '78 and '80 before we won our first championship in 1982. I don't think we did anything much differently when we won the titles as opposed to when we finished second. If anything, we probably focused more on what we did well rather than on the opponent. Teams must prepare for opponents and know their tendencies, but after losing in the championship game three times we realized we had to be primarily concerned with our own play.

Of course, after losing a championship game three times a coach becomes concerned about "choking." That's not a term I like, because it's not fair to the defeated team. The loser of a big game does not necessarily "choke." However, coaches and athletes can't help but doubt themselves a bit after they've lost some big games. Winning that first championship got a big monkey off our back, but coaches must realize some things are out of their control. All they can do is prepare their team as well as possible and let the chips fall.

I learned that lesson in 1979, when my team reached the final eight of the NCAA tournament before losing at Penn State. Our team had 18 shutouts during the season. No NCAA team has ever had more than that. We just dominated our opponents and played beautiful soccer all season, but we ran out of luck at Penn State.

It was one of the most disheartening losses I've had as a coach. We had snow flurries that day, and there was an icy crust on the field. We just couldn't score. It was a game that everyone expected Indiana to win, but we didn't.

It was a tribute to our team, at least, that Penn State carried its goal-keeper off the field. Anytime the opposing team's goalkeeper is the hero of the match, a team knows it did some things right. Their goalkeeper had a magical night, and several of our shots deflected off the posts.

If people had watched that game and not seen the goals, and had then been asked to pick the winner, there's no doubt most of them would have chosen Indiana as the winner. But that's the nature of soccer. Penn State was a great team, too, but I think a lot of people agree that perhaps the nation's top team didn't win the championship that year. That happens in all sports, though, and it usually *evens* out over the long run.

For us, the key to success in the championship games was making it a point to be the aggressor. At Indiana we take great pride in having opponents say they weren't able to *play their game*, that they had a bad day.

That's a great compliment to our team because we stress defense so much. We try to make a team play the way we want them to play, rather than falling back and letting them do what they want to do and trying to stop them at that.

In our third national championship game, against San Francisco in 1980, we concentrated on taking their game away from them. We wanted to determine how the game was going to be played and get the psychological edge on them. We lost that game in overtime, but we were more competitive, and we carried that lesson into our subsequent championship games.

Our loss in the 1980 championship game brought about another challenge: overcoming disappointment. We had a two-goal lead and never expected to lose, but we made a couple of mistakes that allowed them to tie the game. It was our mistakes that cost us, not their big plays. We had nobody to blame for the loss but ourselves. We simply got careless.

First, we knocked in a goal ourselves to give San Francisco their first goal. It started with an errant back pass. One of our players knocked the ball back to our goalkeeper and didn't see they had a player nearby. That began a domino effect. Our other defender came in to try to save the ball and he collided with the goalkeeper and the ball was knocked loose. It could be called a fluke, but we made the fluke occur. We had been completely in control of the game up to that point.

Then, when our heads were still down from giving up a silly goal, two of our players sandwiched one of their players in the penalty area, resulting in a foul and setting up a penalty kick for a goal. There was a direct relationship between the two events. Rather than saying "OK, we made a mistake, let's get our heads up, we're still ahead," we fouled them and suddenly it's 2-2 at halftime.

At halftime I couldn't get their chins up off the floor. It was an incredibly frustrating situation. We thought we had the game won and that we were a much better team, and suddenly we were in trouble. I tried to make the players realize we were still tied, that it was anybody's game. But San Francisco came back out and scored shortly after the start of the second half. We tied the game, 3-3, but later lost in overtime. It was a tough way to lose.

A lot of lessons were learned in that game. First, obviously, a team must be extremely careful about passing the ball back to the goalkeeper. A lot of things can go wrong, as we proved. Beyond that, however, we didn't react

properly to our mistake. We still had a 2-1 lead and were in control of the game after that mistake, but we lost our composure and that led to their second goal. We let it bother us too much, and as a result we didn't come out the second half ready to play.

Experience is another important factor in big games. Aside from the obvious fact that older players usually are more talented, they are also more likely to be poised in pressure situations. This was proven in 1991, when we advanced to the Final Four and played Santa Clara. We had five or six first-year players in the lineup, and they had seven senior starters.

For the first 15 or 20 minutes we played at least even with them. Then they scored on a throw-in in our defensive third of the field. Our players' heads dropped; they weren't mature enough or experienced enough to bounce back from it. Santa Clara's seniors realized that was an opportunity to put us away, and they took control of the game. After that goal we had some opportunities, but for the most part that goal was the turning point. Our team did a great job and overachieved for the most part that season, but the youth and inexperience showed. I think they learned from it.

A coach can't do a lot about situations like these during games. He can't control experience, and he can't call timeouts, so he just has to hope there's enough leadership on the field to meet the challenges. But a coach can't manufacture leadership if it isn't there. All he can do is identify it and allow it to come to the forefront when it is ready to surface.

The importance of leadership was exemplified by one of our players in the early 1980s, John Stollmeyer. It is no coincidence that in the four years he played for us we played in three national championship games, and won two of them. He was more than a great player, he was an inspirational leader. The players feared letting him down as much as they did the coaches.

That kind of leadership is rare, but if a coach is fortunate to have a player with those qualities, he shouldn't be afraid to let him lead. Insecure coaches might worry about giving up part of their authority to a player. That's a mistake. A team needs more leadership than a coach can provide by himself, and there are times — particularly during games — when a leader on the field can do more for the team than a coach can.

• • •

At higher levels of collegiate soccer, substitutions are quite limited. Many times coaches don't make any, and most teams have just two or three players that are used frequently off the bench in close games. Mass substitution is not as prevalent as it is used to be.

In the early years of our program, because our talent didn't match up well with many of our opponents, we had to have our players do a lot more running, so we substituted more. Now that we match up favorably in personnel, we don't substitute much at all.

This means players have to earn their positions in practice. It also means the coach does most of his work in practice, and then the players take over in the games. The coach can still make changes during a game if someone is not playing well. Sometimes making a substitution can change the momentum.

A coach also might have two players very similar in ability who he wants to share playing time. Also, some players — particularly younger players — might not have the fitness level to play 90 minutes. Teams occasionally have situations where they play two or three games a week, or have a weekend tournament in which they play more than one game a day. Some situations demand that more substitutions be made.

Still, at higher levels, teams need to develop a flow, a tempo. This is more difficult to achieve if continuous substitutions are being made. It depends on the level of play, of course. Youth leagues, high schools and some colleges emphasize participation, so coaches at those levels might want to substitute more often. Participation is important, but a better way to guarantee that is to have more teams with fewer players, rather than having a lot of players playing only segments of each game.

We'll have some players on our 25-man roster who go through a season and play very little. That's a difficult situation for them. They have to practice hard like the rest of the team, but they don't get to taste much of the glory. This is an obvious reason not to have a large squad size. It's also a valid justification for having junior varsity games to help keep everyone involved and happy. The players who aren't playing shouldn't be put in a situation where they might damage the entire team's morale. The coach should explain his philosophy to the reserve players and make clear to them their role on the team.

However, we might not start the same 11 players every game. If some-one has a poor game, or is not putting forth the effort in practice, we'll make a change. The bench can be a great motivator for talented players who aren't playing up to their potential. I worry when we have a situation, either because of lack of depth or numerous injuries, where a player feels he can put forth less than his best effort and still remain in the game, or play in the next one.

• • •

One of the great things about coaching is that every season presents a new challenge. It's never the same. It's not a typical 8-5 job. A coach deals with different problems, and must come up with different approaches to motivation and to training. He needs to find ways to keep training activities interesting, challenging and enjoyable. It's difficult for veteran coaches to do that over a long period of time.

It's important for coaches to enjoy what they're doing. That might sound simplistic, but a lot of coaches get burned out and go through the motions, just as players do. If they genuinely love their jobs, however, they should have no problem keeping their emotions high. Coaches who find they have lost their drive and desire should consider moving on to something else.

Every coach has a level where he fits in best. Some work best with beginning players, others with professionals, others somewhere in between. In some part it depends on their personality. I happen to work best with college players.

Every coach should find the level where he is most comfortable and try to work there. It doesn't have to be at the major college or professional level. A coach can have a rewarding career whether he is coaching young kids or high school players. I know I'm glad Barney Hoffman stayed at the high school level. A coach can influence lives at any level, so he shouldn't get hung up on "getting to the top" of the profession. The top is where he is happiest. And the happier he is, the better he will perform as a coach.

I almost left to take a professional coaching job once. It would have paid much more than I was making as a college coach at the time and it seemed like a great opportunity, but it would have been a big mistake for me. At Indiana I'm working with an age group that I enjoy working with and I have a chance to affect their lives and witness the rewards of it. I hear now from guys who played 10 or 15 years ago. They talk about their jobs and their

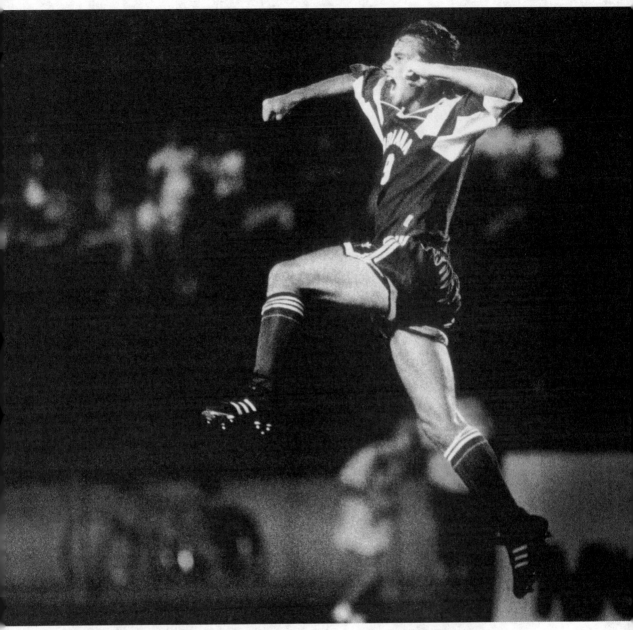

family and sometimes they thank me and tell me how much their participation in the soccer program meant to them, both on the field and off the field.

That, after 30 years of coaching, is as important as what is happening now on the field. I'm as competitive as ever, but the rewards now also come from the products of the program. It's like having children grow up and become successful. That's a great satisfaction for a coach, and shouldn't be taken for granted.

13

Offense

My philosophy toward soccer is very simple. When the opponent has the ball, we want everyone putting 100 percent into defense, both mentally and physically. When we have possession, we want everyone putting 100 percent of their concentration into offense.

As stated in the previous chapter, we want everyone sharing in the attack, with as much interchange as possible. The difficult thing is getting and developing players with the overall skills to play such a system, and then teaching them how to execute it. Obviously, all 10 field players can't be going forward in attack at the same time. Some have to stay back to give the team proper balance and shape. The challenge is to teach them when to go forward and when to stay back. But if a team can generate offense from its back players as well as its front players, it is that much more difficult to defend.

Regardless of a team's offensive style, it should be able to vary the tempo of play. It should be able to build the attack slowly, penetrate quickly and take advantage of what opponents allow. Opponents will defend in different ways, sometimes even during the course of a single game. Coaches must be able to recognize this and take advantage of what's being given. If the opponent allows outside play, for example, or if it allows the backs a great deal of room, the attacking team must be able to react accordingly.

Teams can always learn of an opponent's tendencies from advance scouting, but they must be able to react to changes that occur during games. Players must be trained to do so during practice. Intelligence and recognition are crucial assets for a soccer player.

• • •

Regardless of a team's offensive style, certain principles hold true for most everyone. Two or more team members can create space for themselves through combination play and intelligent movement with and without the ball.

Overlap runs

Overlap runs are made from positions behind the ball. They usually are made from wide positions, near the touch lines, but also can be made in more central locations. The player in possession of the ball must advance slowly, so that the overlapping player can advance around the ballhandler and move toward the live space they are trying to attack.

Communication is important between the two players. The overlapping player must tell the player in possession of the ball to hold the ball while he advances into position. The overlapping player's run should be to the outside of the ballhandler in order to create the best angle for receiving the pass and to give the overlapping player better field vision as he receives the ball.

The player in possession must be careful not to telegraph the pass to the overlapping player by revealing his intention. He also must be careful not to deliver the pass too early or too late. The best time to serve the ball into the attacking space is after the overlapping player comes into the ballhandler's peripheral vision. If the ball is served too late, the overlapping player might be offside; if it is served too soon, the pass might be intercepted.

Takeover plays

Takeover plays are designed to draw two defenders close together, creating confusion and thus creating space for the attackers. Takeover plays can be completed in a side-to-side (across the field) fashion or end-to-end (down the field).

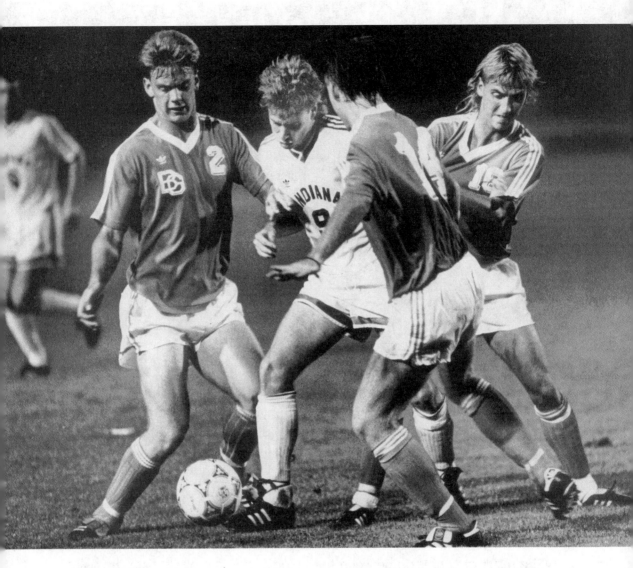

The player in possession of the ball and his teammate move toward each other and cross paths. As they cross, the player not in possession either takes the ball from his teammate or acts as a decoy as his teammate continues to carry the ball into the attack.

The two crossing players must communicate with each other so that they know which of them will have possession of the ball at the moment of the potential takeover. I prefer that the player with the best field of vision determine who keeps possession. This generally is the player not dribbling. If this player determines it is best for him to take possession, he says, "Leave!" as he nears his teammate. If he decides it is best for him not to take possession, he remains silent. Unsuccessful takeover plays usually are the result of confusion between the two players. The player with the ball should leave it for his teammate to pick up rather than try to touch it to him.

It also is important for both players to accelerate at the point of the takeover, regardless of which one has possession. The player with possession as the two players approach must be careful to shield the ball by dribbling with the foot furthest from his opponent.

Penetration

The objective of all attacking teams, unless they are killing the clock, is to move the ball toward the opponent's goal. This is called penetration. To achieve penetration, teams must be able to make forward, positive passes to teammates making hard, accelerated runs into the attacking space.

Early penetration is at the heart of successful counterattacking. The more time the defense is allowed to retreat and get players goalside of the ball, the more difficult it is to make successful penetrating passes. Late penetration often results in failure because the defense has been given time to set up.

Well-timed and early penetrating passes will bypass most defensive players and hopefully result in one-on-one opportunities heading toward goal. It is not always possible to play the ball forward immediately, however, so it is sometimes necessary to play the ball back first to create a better penetrating pass.

The most effective penetrating passes are usually those from a wide position to the center of the field, rather than from the center toward the flank.

Width in attack

A primary objective for any attacking team is to create space. Too often, however, teams become congested in one area of the field and do not take advantage of the width. Spreading out from side to side is one of the best ways to create space and create a more difficult situation for defenders to cover and provide support.

Achieving width enables teams to attack from the flanks toward the center of the field. Players bunching in the center of the field is one of the biggest obstacles coaches face.

Wall pass

The wall pass, also known as the one-two, is a fundamental aspect in attacking play. It is a simple give-and-go maneuver in which a player passes the ball to a teammate, then sprints into an open space to receive a quick return pass.

The maneuver is quite effective, but requires proper timing between the two players. They also must be able to execute the play in close quarters.

The player making the initial pass should try to disguise it. An outside-of-the-foot pass is often the most effective method of doing so. He should make the pass to the wall player's closest foot. He then should immediately accelerate to receive the return pass. The first two steps of the movement, including the foot making the initial pass, are the most important. The second pass is made to space for the first player to run on to.

The wall player also should roll off the defender immediately after passing to the cutting player to try to find space for himself. Too many times the wall player stands and watches, failing to take advantage of an opportunity to receive another return pass.

The passes must be crisp and executed with proper pace. They should be made on the first touch to be effective, and usually are most effectively executed on the ground.

One-touch passing

As players advance to higher levels, they must be able to play accurate one-touch soccer as they close on their opponent's goal. Many golden scoring opportunities are missed because the receiving player must make an extra touch to control the ball. Players must be able to see the field and make an early decision so that they know what they will do with the ball before they receive it.

One-touch (or first-time) play encourages players to constantly survey the field and make decisions before they receive the ball, as well as to keep moving so that they will be in position to receive a pass.

It is important to change the point of attack through a series of one-touch interpassing. The defense cannot react nearly as quickly to a ball passed in one-touch fashion as they can to a player who is dribbling the ball. One-touch passing also requires players to move into proper supporting positions very quickly to help the player receiving the ball. It also encourages and requires players to move into new supporting positions as soon as they have played the ball.

One-touch play is not popular among most players because it is both physically and mentally demanding. Ample practice time should be devoted to improving one-touch skills.

Mobility and blind-side runs

To successfully attack concentrated defenses, players must be mobile and unpredictable. Attacking players make a defender's job relatively easy if they remain stationary in front of the defender. Being creative individually by finding ways to get through the defense with unexpected moves is an important element of improvisation. The great attackers find ways to beat a defense when no openings appear available. It's a spontaneous move that isn't planned and perhaps not even practiced, but draws upon the player's skill and instinct.

Blind-side runs are a common method of executing unpredictable maneuvers. Movement made behind the defense away from the ball places defenders under intense pressure, and can open up space for the attackers.

Blind-side runs are generally instinctive moves made according to what the defense allows. If defenders focus too much on play around the ball — get caught ball-watching — and lose track of other attackers, they leave themselves vulnerable to blind-side runs. Attackers should be looking for every opportunity to slip behind their marker and find open space to receive a pass.

An effective blind-side run in the attacking third requires the runner to have good vision and timing, as well as the ability to finish. Blind-side runs are effective maneuvers in any area of the field, however. They are most commonly made from the flank toward the center of the field, but can be made diagonally from the center toward the flank.

Runners must remember that their efforts often will not bring a pass. The player in possession of the ball might not see the runner in time to make a pass, if he sees him at all, or the ballhandler might choose to make another play. Still, players must be willing to make runs whenever they are appropriate. Even if they do not receive a pass, they can contribute to the attack by stretching the defense and creating an opening for a teammate. Even the mere threat of a blind-side run can assist the attack because it keeps the defense spread wider, thus increasing the chances of finding open attacking space.

● ● ●

I prefer that my teams play a short passing, ball control game, keeping the ball on the ground but mixing in direct play utilizing quick penetrating ability. That's not unusual, but to try to impose such a style on players who are not prepared for it can be very frustrating. Coaches can try to encourage and develop a certain style of play, but they must first determine what the players are capable of doing and try to build from there.

In my early years as a coach, when we did not have great talent, we were a defensive-oriented, counterattacking team. We generated much of our attack by inviting the opponent to attack us, forcing them into mistakes and countering quickly. We didn't have the talent to match up all over the field with our opponents then, but we did have good speed up front.

We used that tactic when Angelo DiBernardo, a freshman, scored five goals against St. Louis in 1976. Nobody had ever scored five goals against St. Louis before. The game was played on artificial turf in our football stadium, so that catered to his speed.

Sixty to 70 percent of that game was played in our defensive half, with St. Louis in control of the ball, and yet we scored five counterattack goals. Angelo stayed up top, while our defense didn't allow them high percentage scoring chances. As soon as we won the ball we looked for Angelo and got the ball to him in the open field. We kept him at midfield, as his job was to be in the best position on the receiving end of a penetrating pass as soon as we won possession. As a result, we were able to get him one-on-one against a defender in a foot race to goal.

Today we play a different style because we have better overall talent, but DiBernardo was truly gifted and we wanted to take advantage of his ability. We wanted to give the opponent a false sense of security by inviting them into our half of the field and then give Angelo the entire half of the field to attack against one or two defenders.

In those days we were trying to generate a lot of our offense off the other team's mistakes. This is a suitable strategy for teams that are outmanned by their opponent. Now, because we have better talent and can match up with our opponents, we try to dictate how we want to play on offense and change the tempo depending on what the opponents give us.

That's part of the chess game, seeing what is available that day and taking advantage of it, while trying to take away the opponent's favored style of play. Our midfielders and backs now contribute up to 50 percent of our scoring, while in our early days 90 percent of our scoring came from our front players.

Coaches must assess their players' skills and potential, and then determine how they should generate the attack. Trying to mount a counterattack as the primary offensive tactic is foolish if a team does not have extremely quick players up front. The speed of the front players determines to a large extent if a team will be successful using the counterattack tactic.

Our current approach to offense, which incorporates everyone into the offense, paid off in 1982, when Gregg Thompson, a defender, scored both of our goals in a 2-1, eight-overtime win over Duke in the national championship game. Gregg was one of our best defenders and he was marking one of Duke's top scorers, but when we had the ball he was expected to join the attack at the appropriate time.

He scored a great goal off of a throw-in from about 20 yards out. Then he scored on a free kick to win the game in the eighth overtime. Gregg practiced that free kick everyday. It didn't happen by chance.

He was a great role model and inspiration for our other players. Gregg came to practice earlier, stayed later and worked harder than the others so that when his chance did come he'd be ready for it. It did come, and he was ready. He went on to become the NASL Rookie of the Year and played for the United States in the 1984 Olympics.

As a coach, it's a tremendous thrill seeing guys like that succeed, because they deserve every bit of the success they get. Gregg Thompson served as an excellent role model to everyone because of his strong work ethic. He didn't have great size, but he worked hard at weight training and became very strong. And his work ethic toward skill development — in this case the free kick — paid off handsomely.

We had a similar situation occur in our 1983 championship win over Columbia, when Pat McGauley scored the only goal of the game in the second overtime. Pat had gone through a scoring drought at the end of the season. He was one of our key forwards, but he was struggling. A lot of players would have gotten down on themselves and let it affect their play, but he hung in there. He worked through the drought and put forth the extra effort to score the game-winner.

This a lesson for all players regarding persistence. No matter how talented a player is, he is bound to have slumps. However, he can't let it affect his intensity or confidence. And coaches must have patience with players who are struggling, as long as they have proven their talent in the past. We had been telling Pat he was going to get a goal when it really counted, and he did. He put forth a great deal of effort to reach a cross that wasn't certain of even getting through to him.

● ● ●

A team's playing style might need to change during a game, depending on the situations that arise. A team that is leading with 10 or 15 minutes to go, for example, should not take unnecessary risks. Perhaps it commits fewer players to its attack to help avoid exposing itself and allowing a possible scoring opportunity for the other team. Teams should know how to kill the clock.

At the same time, teams must be careful when they have the lead to continue playing to win, rather than playing not to lose. The team with the lead can't just sit back. It must continue to play aggressively and positively, but avoid putting itself at risk. The shift in playing style when a team has the lead should be minor, not drastic.

Teams that are behind need to be able to make adjustments as well. Something we do is go "even numbers" by playing without our sweeper. We did that in 1984 in the championship game when we were trailing 1-0 with about 15 minutes remaining. We had prepared for this type of situation in practice. By pulling a sweeper out and putting another player in, we were able to go head-to-head with the opponent all over the field. We were able to force some turnovers, then we drew a foul, got a free kick and tied the score 1-1.

We also go even numbers if we aren't generating offense during a game and we need to create a change in momentum. It is important to remember, however, that a team makes itself more vulnerable to conceding a goal by removing the sweeper.

If a team is trailing, but generating good scoring opportunities, there is no need to go even numbers until about 15 minutes remain in the game. If a team is not generating offense, however, it might be wise to go to it earlier.

Weather conditions and the field surface can also cause a change in playing style. Wind, rain, snow, hard ground, soft ground, the size of the field, the height of the grass, artificial turf — all these are conditions that can affect how a team approaches the game.

If a team is playing on a heavy field or a wet field, it might be advantageous to go to a more direct game, with more long passes and less dribbling and short passes. Some coaches whose teams are more effective when playing at a slow tempo have been known to keep the grass on their field a bit higher to help slow down play. Artificial turf, on the other hand, favors teams with superior running speed.

Teams playing on a windy day should try to keep the ball out of the air, or take advantage of the conditions by putting the ball up near the opponent's goal area if they have tall people who can dominate there.

Games on a narrow field might force teams to play a more direct style, with the ball in the air more. Teams that play on high school football fields don't have much width to work with, which makes it difficult to open up combination play through the midfield.

• • •

When a team gains possession of the ball, its players should initially read how the opponent is defending and take advantage of what is available. Everyone must concentrate on how they can take the situation and turn it to their advantage as quickly as possible. Where should they be moving without the ball? Where should they be moving to provide support?

If you are playing a team that gives you even numbers — for example, one that plays without a deep sweeper and does not have good cover in the back — you must recognize this and try to serve the ball to your front players, who can go one-on-one.

If your opponent uses zone principles, then your players should play the ball more to each other's feet and change the point of attack quickly. Zone defense allows that space of three or four yards when players are moving from one zonal area to the next. Against a zone, players must work hard to find blind side positions to open the space they need to receive the ball.

When playing against a team employing strict man-to-man defense, players should make unselfish runs to create space for other players who are not tightly marked. Players also must work hard at running their defenders into less dangerous space, space that they do not want to exploit, to open up space in front of the opponent's goal, and then find ways to serve the ball to teammates in that area.

A team cannot go into a game and simply say, "We're going to play our game." If a team is that much better than its opponent it might be able to do that, but at higher levels of play it is not a practical approach. When teams are roughly equal in talent, players must recognize what's being given to them.

A team should not try to force balls to its front players if it has two front players against four back players. On the other hand, it shouldn't try to build up slowly if it is given even numbers up front; in such a situation it must play the ball forward and penetrate early.

Ideally, a team will be versatile in its offensive approach and be able to do what the game dictates: build up, play direct, come from behind, or create space for front, midfield or back players.

If a team is unfamiliar with its opponent, the first 10 to 15 minutes of a match is a sparring process, a time to sort out what type of defense it is up against. Whichever team can establish the tempo of play generally will be successful.

If a team is struggling against an opponent's defense, individual creativity might help it overcome the situation. If the defense allows space for the backs to operate and then suddenly cuts it off, for example, it would be foolish to try to keep forcing the ball out of the back. Against Hartwick in the semifinal of the 1984 NCAA tournament, and then against Clemson in the final, our backs did not have the opportunity to build out of the back; both teams had devised defenses that kept them out of our attack. That meant, however, that we had players open in the midfield. We recognized that a little too late in the final game against Clemson, which we lost 2-1, but we made some adjustments at halftime and were able to generate some strong attacks.

Players must be willing to take risks in the offensive third of the field. They are likely to be up against even numbers or perhaps an extra defender there, so individual creativity is an important asset. Players must be willing to challenge defenders and risk losing possession in the offensive third of the field.

The principles of improvisation — doing the unexpected — come into play here. There is less space to work in, so a team's offensive options are limited. Top attackers can unbalance the defense by beating their defender, then draw the extra player (the sweeper) to give their team even numbers — which usually is all any team can hope for in attack.

Players must assume the responsibility of attempting to beat players one-on-one, and coaches must assume the responsibility of training their players against numbers that favor the defense. Practice time should be devoted to getting the ball behind the defense on the flanks and then serving balls to both the near and far post, on the ground and in the air.

The timing of runs is another important phase of attack, and should receive considerable attention in practice. Players without the ball must learn when to make their move. Players must learn in practice how to communicate during games, either by word or by signal to coordinate attacking runs.

Too often players are caught standing in front of the goal in the space their team wants to attack, which is almost like giving the opponent another defender. This is a common problem with younger players. Players should be in a good striking position on the field prepared to make a run at the proper speed and appropriate time so that the players arrive simultaneously with the ball.

Of course all the runs in the world won't do a team any good if its players cannot make the proper service, and practice time should be devoted to this skill as well.

• • •

The interchangeable offensive style I prefer requires a great deal of movement from our players. First, however, the players must be taught about proper movement. Sometimes coaches stand on the touch line yelling, "Move! Move!" As a result the players are running around like crazy with no purpose, wasting a lot of energy because they're moving at the wrong time, to the wrong place and at the wrong speed. There's nothing wrong with players pacing themselves by standing, walking or jogging at times, but when a run is made it must be made with a purpose and at an accelerated speed.

Communication through eye contact is crucial to good offensive play. If a player makes a run but his teammate with the ball has his head down, the runner is wasting his time and effort. This is where one of the most basic fundamentals comes into play: keep your head up while dribbling.

When the dribbler's head comes up and eye contact is achieved, that's the time to make the run. A run not only creates an opportunity for the player making it, it takes defenders away from teammates and creates opportunities for them as well. A player indirectly can assist his teammates by being a "sacrificial" runner.

Some players are great at making runs and drawing defenders, then taking them into dead space to open up live space for teammates. Too many players want to make runs only for themselves, so they can receive the ball. Ultimately a great run does both, creating opportunities for the runner and his teammates.

Many times offenses bog down because players stand and want balls played to their feet while being closely marked, or their runs are straight up and down the field. It's a defender's joy to find a player who makes north and south runs. They're easy to track. A defender's nightmare is the player who makes an unpredictable run. It might start forward and then move laterally, or incorporate fakes.

Attacking players must learn to play their defenders into situations where they can beat them with a well-timed run. Too many offensive players let their defender mark them. A good attacker should always be thinking of how he can beat his defender, waiting for the moment when the defender looks away for a split second and then make a run to find open space.

This is where communication and chemistry come into play. Over time, and through practice, players learn to anticipate each other's moves and develop a sixth sense for where their teammates are going to be. This is another argument for full-sided match conditions during practice.

Certain attacking situations in different areas of the field lend themselves to various options. A team can have takeovers, overlap runs and one-two combination plays; it can send a third man through, it can set up near post and far post runs, and it can serve early crosses and late crosses. All of these attacking situations must be practiced to develop proper timing and recognition.

• • •

As stated before, communication is very important on offense, but much of it should be non-verbal. We often set up situations in practice where we don't allow the attacking players to talk, even in full-sided scrimmages. Players tend to get lazy and restrict their field of vision; they want to hear where their teammates are.

The problem here is the first call from a teammate might work, but the second one is going to tip off the defender for sure. Much of the talking players do while on offense is selfish talking — a player asking for the ball.

If a player finds space to receive a pass, the minute he opens his mouth he's informing the defender of his location. By being forced to remain silent during practice, the ballhandler assumes the responsibility for knowing the whereabouts of his teammates.

Coaches also can enforce the condition that players cannot call for the ball to be served to themselves. Allow the players to only give verbal direction for a player to pass to someone else. Many times three or four players are yelling at the ballhandler to pass them the ball.

Communication offensively should come from behind. If a wide back is in possession, his sweeper should be able to see the field and provide direction, rather than having a front runner call for the ball. The sweeper should be calling out direction such as "Wide to Mike!" to help the ball-handler, rather than yelling "Pass it back to me!"

When midfielders have the ball, the defenders behind them should be offering verbal instruction. They can see who's open. Too many times the communication is coming from the advanced players who are working hard to free themselves, and they spoil their effort by calling attention to themselves.

Hopefully by the time a team gets into an actual game, the communication process has been sorted out and the players know when to talk and what to say. Nothing frustrates and panics a player more than to hear several teammates yelling for the ball. This is something younger players in particular need to work on. Kids have a natural instinct to call for the ball.

• • •

If a coach is fortunate, he will have players from time to time who are blessed with exceptional attacking skills. He then must decide what limits, if any, to put on them. One extreme is to try to inhibit their style so they fit in with the rest of the team. The other extreme is to give them a totally free reign and let them do as they please, even at the expense of the team.

I believe one of the beautiful aspects of soccer is the individual flair players exhibit. It's thrilling when a truly gifted player gets the ball and the spectators know something exciting is going to happen.

Coaches should encourage more individual creativity. Coaches have traditionally emphasized getting rid of the ball, discouraging players from trying to create opportunities on their own. But if a player has exceptional skill, he shouldn't be harnessed too much.

In basketball, players such as Michael Jordan, Isiah Thomas and Magic Johnson could take over a game on their own. Every time they got the ball fans were on the edge of their seats waiting for something to happen. I don't think it's a coincidence that all three of those players starred on teams that won at least two championships in the National Basketball Association in the 1980s. However, we have a shortage of players like that in soccer because we haven't encouraged that kind of individual flair.

This isn't to say team play should be ignored. Just as Thomas, Johnson and Jordan stayed within the framework of team play, so must soccer players. It's still a team game, so any individual play has to come within the team framework. If a player goes one-on-one every time he gets the ball, his team will suffer for it.

Players with a magical flair should be encouraged to use it, but only for the good of the team. Good players who have the ability and the flair to unbalance a defense should recognize when they've drawn two or three defenders and lay off the pass and let the other guy get the easy goal. They shouldn't do the work just for themselves.

Sometimes younger players who are standouts on their team — or *believe* they are — think they have to dribble everytime they receive the ball. They do their hard work for themselves, not for the benefit of the team. Developing the proper recognition of the game is an important part of a younger player's development. I've had some great dribblers who frustrated their teammates and in some ways stifled our attack because they didn't recognize when they should get rid of the ball. They didn't read the game.

A key factor in successful one-on-one encounters is that the offensive player must try to attack the defender head-on — not go around or away from him, but right at him. Speed is the attacker's best weapon. However, players must realize that they cannot always approach defenders at the same speed. They need to save an extra gear to accelerate by varying their speed.

Coaches cannot teach a player individual flair, however. Nobody ever sat down with Pele or any of the other great ones and explained to them how to make the moves they made. They developed their own moves, sometimes on the spot. That was part of their genius. They practiced basic moves to develop better ball control and learn the fundamentals, but they acquired and perfected their own subtle moves.

What coaches can do is set up practice so that players are encouraged to develop their own moves. He can, for example, give awards or recognition for the best move to help create an atmosphere that encourages players to work on the individual aspects of their games. It's important to remember that a player doesn't need five or six moves; one effective move with a counter move is all that is really necessary. A lot of defenders have been familiar with the favorite moves of the great players, but that didn't mean they could stop them.

Small-sided scrimmages, from one-on-one to six-on-six, are effective methods of teaching players to enhance their individual skills. Smaller numbers should be used if there's a restriction, such as one-touch. A smaller playing area, such as 40 × 40, can be used, and it might be helpful to use more than one ball.

Coaches also can set conditions for attackers, such as requiring them to beat a defender before shooting. Have them create an opportunity with a dribbling move, or create an opportunity for a teammate by beating their man and then finding the open man. They should beat one defender, draw the second one, and then lay off a pass to a teammate.

Coaches also can set up exercises realistic to a game where two attackers go up against three defenders — two markers and one supporting player — and the attackers have to create opportunities through combination play and creative individual moves.

Many times coaches set up drills that give the numerical advantage to the attack, such as a three-on-two or two-on-one. Howver, it's more likely that attackers will face one-on-two, two-on-three or three-on-four situations. Coaches should structure their training to resemble more realistic game situations, where their attackers must be able to hold the ball and create opportunities on their own against a defensive numerical advantage.

• • •

Coaches also should emphasize a finish (a shot on goal) as often as possible in practice. This aspect of training is often ignored, as some coaches are content on working to improve dribbling and passing skills.

This also relates to why we haven't developed more soccer players in the United States with the magical scoring ability of a Pele. We have not, in the United States, developed *goal scorers* compared to other soccer cultures. American players can control the ball and pass the ball, and are physically able to compete, but in the offensive third of the field they don't have the sophistication and the composure that players from other countries have. Too many American players lose their composure when they get in scoring position. They feel rushed, and rather than relishing the opportunity to score, they squander it.

Again, coaches can enhance the finishing ability of their players by placing them in scoring opportunities more often during practice. To not do so is like a basketball coach having his players pass the ball for 45 minutes during practice, and then have them take only three or four shots before heading for the showers. In basketball, kids have been shooting hoops since they were big enough to dribble a basketball. Soccer players, however, aren't likely to have a soccer goal in their backyard, so they are more likely to work on ballhandling skills.

The objective of soccer, however, is to score. That objective should be included, with full-sized goals and goalkeepers, in as many activities as possible. Almost *every* exercise, whether it is one-on-one or a full scrimmage, should include a finish as a major focus of the activity, not an afterthought. Ideally, a team has several goalkeepers, so that when it separates into smaller groups it still can include a shot on goal with each activity.

Through proper experience gained from practice, players are less likely to panic when they have a scoring opportunity in a game. This not only applies to forwards, but to all players. Too often a player tries to pass the responsibility off to someone else when he is in a good scoring position.

Goalkeepers also benefit when finishing situations are made game-like. They do not benefit as much when someone kicks still balls off the ground at them. The ball should be struck on goal while rolling, bouncing or while in the air. Coaches must always think back to the game and develop shooting exercises that resemble the situations that arise there.

Balls should be served to attacking players from behind, such as a midfielder giving a through ball to a forward, from crosses and from in front, as in a rebound or when a player delivers a pass from the end line. The serves should come on the ground and in the air.

Players can practice these situations without defense at first to improve their technique and speed, then opposition can be added to make it more functional.

• • •

Attitude also is a major factor in developing finishing skills. So many times, coaches stress passing and teamwork to the extent that shooting is downplayed. If a shot misses, the player receives negative reinforcement. Players must realize that not attempting to score is a greater mistake than missing a shot. They need to be encouraged to overcome fear of failure.

I believe a player who misses a shot on goal or loses the ball when attempting to beat someone at the proper time should be praised by his coach and teammates for a good effort. Players must be willing to take a risk at the appropriate times. A player cannot be discouraged by failure. The good forward might have the ball taken away from him nine times when he's trying to go to goal, but the 10th time he gets through. If he loses his confidence or worries about what his coach or teammates might say after failing a few times, he will have a very difficult time scoring.

It makes more sense to constructively criticize a player who fails to attempt an opportunity when it is available, whether it involves taking a shot or taking on a defender. Not to take the chance at all is far worse than taking it and failing. Of course the willingness to take risks should increase as a player nears the opponent's goal.

My philosophy is that the best players often make the most mistakes, basically because they're trying to accomplish positive things. In baseball, Reggie Jackson struck out 2,597 times, more than anyone in the history of the game. But people aren't likely to remember that. They probably remember that he hit 563 home runs. In soccer, a coach should allow his "home run hitters" to "strike out" on occasion. A player who comes to me after the game and says, "I had a perfect game; I didn't lose the ball once," doesn't impress me. That player might as well have been on the other team, because he probably played it much too safe. He made square passes or back passes, never took a run forward with the ball, and rarely put himself in position to fail.

I'm not advocating a "fools rush in" attitude, but I want players to be aggressive in their approach and take some risks. This involves the ability to make proper reads and early decisions with good vision, and that's one of the hardest things to develop. Players tend to want to watch the ball, receive the ball, control the ball, have some touches and *then* look up to see what to do.

The soccer players with great attacking skills know before they receive the ball what they're going to do with it. People said Pele had *eyes* in the back of his head. Actually, his head was moving all the time when he didn't have the ball. He was like a banty rooster. When the ball came he had already taken all the pictures of the field and knew what needed to be done. He knew where his teammates were and where the defense was coming from.

This is one of the hardest elements to coach. When people refer to a player as being "skillful", many times they really mean that he has outstanding ball control. Skill also involves being able to use that ball control at the proper time and place by reading the game before receiving the ball.

What a coach *can* do is ask players to look up ahead of time and learn to read the game. We do that by playing one- touch in exercises, or perhaps two-touch or three-touch. If a coach asks the players what they least like to work on in practice, most of them would say one-touch or two-touch, because they have to use their brain. If they have to play one-touch, they're going to have to work hard at recognizing what's on before they receive the ball.

We have had several players with very good technique, and who were able to take full advantage of their skills by reading the game. But we also have had players who were not very intelligent from a soccer standpoint. They had a difficult time reading the game, and as a result made late decisions and improper decisions. Much of that is due to the fact they play within a very small field, so to speak. They play on a 10-yard field, rather than a 75 × 120 field. They see what's in their little area, but other than that they don't know what's going on. We have to broaden that focus, broaden their vision and make them more soccer intelligent. This is a challenge, but it can be done.

I remember one player in particular who was very technically sound and athletic, but just didn't see the field. He was able to beat people because of his athletic ability and skillful ball control — he was even able to play professionally for awhile — but his talent was like the tip of an iceberg. He never reached his potential because he did not improve his reading of the game and did not become a skillful player in the true sense.

It's frustrating for a coach to see talent like that wasted. We tried everything we could, and improved his recognition some, but not as much as was needed. This is something many coaches don't spend enough time on, working with players in learning to read the game.

Video helps teach players to have better vision. A coach can tell a player over and over again that he's not seeing the field, but if together they can review the player's performance on tape it helps get the point across.

• • •

One of my favorite activities for developing offensive skills is a small-sided, three-on-three transition game. This exercise can accomplish many objectives, including the following:

- It exposes a player who does not work hard to get open. Many times when a player complains that he's not getting the ball enough it's his own fault because he's unable to find open space. No matter how good a player's offensive abilities are, if he cannot get himself into open space he is not going to be successful.
- It highlights players who know when and how to take on defenders.
- Using a 40-yard field with keepers and full-size goals, it shows which players can finish and which players need work on that part of their game.
- It shows which players are best at making immediate transition from defense to offense, and vice-versa, and exposes players who want to stand and watch when a change in possession occurs.
- It requires tight ball control and proper combination play in close quarters.

The three-on-three exercise can be utilized with various conditions. It can be done without forced marking, allowing the defenders to provide support, switch men or double-team. However, it also is effective when restricted one-on-one situations are enforced. Time should also be devoted to situations in which the defense has the numerical advantage to better simulate game conditions.

⚽14
Defense

To say that defense wins championships is a cliché, but it can be true. We allowed only one goal in our championship game in 1982, and allowed none in '83 and '88. We were able to control the ball a fair amount of time in these games, and at the same time we were able to stop our opponents when they were on the attack.

Defense has been the common thread of our program over the years. We haven't always had great attacking teams, but we've consistently played well defensively. That's because of the emphasis we place on defense and the attention we devote to it during practice.

In the early years of our program when soccer was a club sport, and then when it first became a varsity sport in 1973, we naturally didn't have an abundance of talented players. We were able to be competitive, though, because of our emphasis on defense. A great deal of our attack originated from our defense in those years. Although we have more attacking talent available today, we still take a great deal of pride in how well we defend.

I tell our players they're going to work harder on defense here than they ever have before. We find that some of the so-called "prima donna" players coming out of high school were given special liberties and aren't used to playing defense. They need a little attitude adjustment in regard to their work ethic and focus when the other team has possession of the ball.

However, these players soon learn that it's worth it. I believe the commitment we make to defense is one of the primary reasons a good number of our players have gone on to play professionally over the years. They've been able to compete with some of the more experienced international players because they are disciplined defensively. A sound defensive player can contribute to a team even if he doesn't have great offensive skills.

Good defensive play can be a great equalizer. It can make up for lack of offensive talent, to a degree, and it can cover for a team when the attack bogs down. Every team has the occasional game when it just can't buy a goal, days when its shots hit the goal post or it comes up against a hot goalkeeper. Excellent defense can pull a team through on these occasions.

● ● ●

Defense can be approached in different ways from a philosophical standpoint. This is most evident in World Cup play. The Germans utilize close man marking principles, which combines well with their aggressive attacking style. Other countries are geared more toward a zone defense. The Italians, for example, often fall back and get numbers up near their goal, and then generate offense through counterattack. Other countries play a defense that combines elements of both man-to-man and zone.

All defenses fall into the categories of a man-to-man marking system or a zone, or some combination of the two. Both systems have their advantages and disadvantages, and one could argue on behalf of either one.

The advantages of the man marking system include the following:

- Defenders can be matched up against an opponent's specific attacking strengths to neutralize their effectiveness.
- Individual defensive responsibilities are more easily defined and understood.
- An opponent's attacking weaknesses can be identified and exploited more easily.
- Specific problem areas are more recognizable and can be corrected more readily during a game.
- Time and space are more effectively eliminated from the opponent.

The disadvantages of the man marking system include the following:

- It is extremely demanding, both physically and mentally.
- It generally requires the use of a free back or sweeper, which is a specialized skill.
- Players executing a strict man-to-man system tend to be reluctant to go forward in attack out of fear of neglecting their defensive assignment.
- Providing support and depth can be more difficult, and players can become more isolated in their defensive roles. This leaves defenders facing an unfavorable matchup at greater risk.

A zone defense can be executed in one of several ways. Teams can play a high-pressure system that puts pressure on the ball, or fall back into a more conservative zone that places more players near their goal, with just one or two pressuring the ball.

Regardless of the approach, the advantages of a zone defense include the following:

- Players are responsible for areas of the field rather than specific players, which makes it easier to teach and more flexible.
- It is less physically and mentally demanding on each player.
- The defense can overload areas near its goal to make it more difficult for the opponent to score.
- It helps neutralize individual mismatches.
- The players generally feel as if they have more freedom to attack.
- It is easier for the defenses to stay more compact and not get stretched by the attacking team.

The disadvantages of the zone defense include:

- Attackers are allowed time and space when they move from one defensive zone to another.
- Communication can break down between defenders as attackers are switched from one zone to another, particularly if the defenders have not played together for a long period of time.
- Players tend to lose mental concentration, and are more prone to cheat at their work ethic because they are not individually exposed.
- It is more difficult to identify (and therefore correct) individual breakdowns.
- It can put players in a more passive frame of mind, which might affect their aggressiveness toward attacking.

• • •

At Indiana, one of our most emphasized defensive elements is to not play negatively by falling back and reacting to what the opponent wants to do. We strive to play aggressive, "positive" defense by trying to establish how our opponent will play and then working hard to stop it. Teams become frustrated if they are not allowed to do the things they are accustomed to doing offensively.

The greatest compliment a team can receive after a game is to have the opponent say, "We just didn't play our game today. It wasn't our day." That's another way of saying they were well-defended. Any opponent can play well if it is allowed to do what it wants to do. The idea is to take a team out of its favored style of play.

To do this requires a number of important factors. Three of the major defensive objectives are as follows:

- Recover ball possession as quickly as possible in a location closer to the opponent's goal than your own. This means your players must be more fit, more disciplined and more devoted to defense than the opponent.
- Allow the opponent only back, square or negative passes, not penetrating passes directed toward your goal. To do so, teams must apply tight pressure.
- Force opponents to take shots on goal from low percentage angles and distance after they reach the attacking third of the field.

I believe a man-to-man marking system accomplishes these defensive objectives more effectively. The primary problem I find with a zone defense is that it leaves the attacking team with too many opportunities to find openings as its players move from one defender's zone to another.

We do not, however, play a strict man marking system. In a strict man marking system, individual marking assignments are followed throughout the game. We use what I call the "most dangerous man" marking system. For example, we don't ask No. 3 on our team to always mark No. 9 on the opposing team. If No. 3 on our team goes up in attack and No. 9 on their team stays back, No. 3 would have to run all the way back to find No. 9 when we lose the ball. That's very demanding and often stifles a player's offensive contribution because he is too concerned about getting back on defense.

It is much better for players to be able to interchange defensive assign-ments so that they can get into the attack more quickly. Our defensive philosophy, therefore, is that when possession is lost, the players mark the most dangerous player on the other team closest to them. No. 3, who has been up in attack, would then find the most dangerous opponent closest to him at the instant the opposing team gains possession of the ball.

It is important for defenders to be patient and not leave their man to pick up a less dangerous opponent who has the ball. Defenders never should leave the man they are marking unless another opponent becomes more dangerous. The sweeper must provide good direction in order to maintain defensive balance and shape so that an unmarked opponent does not become a scoring threat. Disciplined man-to-man marking principles must be followed so that players do not get blind-sided or lose sight of opponents away from the ball.

A key that determines success both offensively and defensively is *rec-ognition on transition and immediate communication and adjustment.* We work very hard on this.

For example, if No. 3 is close to two players from the opposing team, he must quickly decide which man to mark and communicate his decision to his teammates. That's where the sweeper must contribute in sorting out the marking. He is the coach on the field, and must constantly be com-municating with his teammates. The goalkeeper must help in this regard, too. Their teammates, in turn, must be willing to listen.

This system demands that all players be able to defend well. The front players and midfielders will at times find themselves marking attacking players, so it is crucial that they develop sound defensive techniques to go with their offensive skills. Defenders generally will be in the same vicinity as their opposing attackers, but they also will need to interchange from front to back and laterally.

Occasionally teams might face an opponent with a player who is such a great scoring threat that the coach assigns one player to defend that player exclusively. He sacrifices his player's offensive contribution in this case, therefore such a move should be done only in extreme circumstances. The defender would shadow his man all over the field, and not leave him even when his team has the ball. This strategy does not mean the other players can relax on defense.

Sometimes coaches allow their most gifted offensive players to rest when the other team has the ball. They don't require them to mentally or physically devote themselves to defense because they're saving themselves for attack. I don't believe, however, that a team can have a prima donna forward resting on defense. That places an added burden on the other players. If everybody shares the load and maintains the philosophy that they are defending as a team, each player has an important defensive role to play.

This philosophy has been one of the major reasons for our success over the years. We've worked very hard on the individual and team principles of defense, and we insist that everyone share the load and work hard for each other.

An offshoot of this philosophy is that it builds better team unity. If coaches allow certain "glamour" players to relax on defense and avoid the dirty work, other players are likely to resent it, and that can have a negative effect on the team's performance. If everyone shares responsibilities and opportunities, it helps create a better overall team atmosphere.

• • •

Although the ultimate objective of the defending team is to regain possession of the ball, it is important not to lose sight of another important priority: stopping the opponent from scoring. Regardless of a team's specific approach, certain defensive principles apply in achieving this dual objective.

Pressurizing

The act of limiting the space and time an attacker has to play the ball, pressurizing should begin the instant ball possession is lost. It is at this very moment many players lose concentration and are most vulnerable to attack.

Pressurizing distance should be as close as possible, ideally one to two yards. Players also should be goalside of the ball so that an attacker cannot make penetrating, positive passes or attempt a clear shot on goal.

Inexperienced players tend to pressurize more loosely because they are afraid of getting beat. This is a vital mistake, because it gives the attacking player time and space to pick his options, whether it be to dribble, pass or shoot.

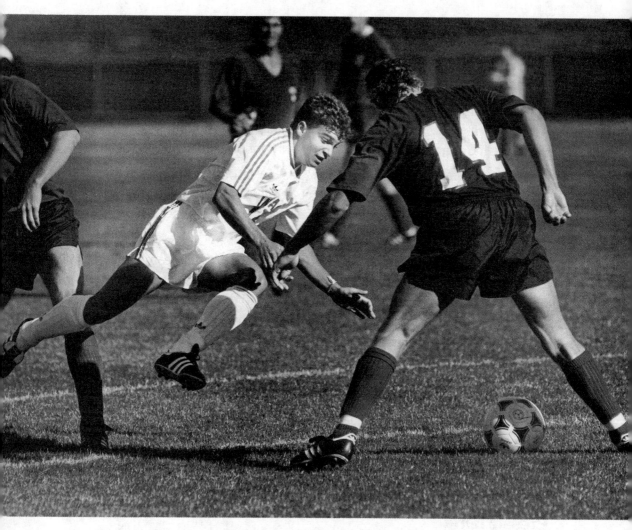

At Indiana, we attempt to force our opponents' scoring opportunities to come from at least 20 yards. Teams obviously have a better chance to stop shots from longer distances and from poor angles. It is wise to monitor the types of shots opponents are generating. This is done easily through videotaping and charting each scoring opportunity.

Support and depth

Defenses restrict the space between defenders and behind defenders away from the ball through the process of support and depth. Proper supporting depth and angles must be taught; they vary depending on the speed and ability of the attacker, the location of the ball, the position on the field and the location of the other defenders.

Generally, the supporting defender away from the ball should be no more than five yards from his opponent. He should be as close as two yards when the attacker reaches shooting distance. The definition of "shooting distance" depends on the ability of the attacker, but it generally is the edge of the penalty area. The proper angle for the supporting defender is generally 45 degrees, but this also depends on the body position of the pressurizing defender.

The supporting player must also pass on proper information to the pressurizing player, such as whether he should commit to the tackle and which direction he should attempt to jockey the ballhandler.

Compactness

Defenses must stay compact and avoid being stretched too far, both front to back and side to side. Teams that do not remain compact allow too much space to the opposing team, and it becomes very difficult to properly pressurize and provide support.

Communication

Proper communication is vital to good defensive play. The supporting players must communicate with their teammates to let them know where they are and to instruct them on what they might not be able to see.

The sweeper and goalkeeper must be the primary communicators because of their positions on the field, but all players must take responsibility in the communication process that weaves a defense together. Players should be encouraged to talk during practice to develop the habit, although there is nothing like actual game competition to hone a team's communication skills.

My 1979 team that had 18 shutouts in 22 games probably communicated with each other better than any team I've coached. That team had seven seniors, and they had played together for a few years. Veteran players tend to have a better understanding of each other and the game, and tend to be more confident. As a result, they usually are better communicators.

Communication also helps establish mental discipline and control on defense, and helps keep panic from setting in. Players are less likely to let down if teammates are offering them support and encouragement.

Delay and cover

When a team loses possession of the ball, players must get goalside of the ball quickly to blunt the opponent's attack. During this process, pressurizing players try to delay the attack by jockeying and shepherding ballhandlers into less dangerous areas of the field, such as the touch line, so that all defenders can get into proper supporting positions and avoid a numerical disadvantage.

Patience on the part of the defender pressurizing the ballhandler is necessary in this situation. If he overcommits on a tackling attempt and fails, he places the rest of the defenders in jeopardy.

Players on the "weak" side, or away from, the ball should take the quickest recovery route to the danger area and then determine their best strategy. It might be to challenge for the ball, delay the player with the ball, mark another attacker or provide support.

This process should involve the entire team, not just the backs. Teams that effectively drop back in an intelligent and well-executed manner not only delay the attack by marking the attacker's forwards, they improve their chance of frustrating the attacking team and regaining possession of the ball.

This process is largely a matter of hustle. By getting back into a proper position quickly, the defense can prevent the attacking team from gaining the numerical advantage it seeks. It comes down to knowing where to go and getting there quickly.

As a team retreats, it should do so in a funneling pattern toward goal (see illustration on page 66), therefore concentrating the defenders toward the middle of the field. The concentration should become more compact as it nears the goal.

Tracking

This is particularly important in a man marking system. Defenders must be able to track opponents who are not in possession of the ball, while keeping the ball in view at all times. They cannot put themselves in a blind side position by being a ball watcher and losing track of the attacker they are marking. This is an important skill and requires discipline and concentration as well as proper positioning.

Defenders should be able to see the ball and their man at all times. They should position themselves to intercept a pass that might come to their man, make a tackle as their man receives the ball, or prevent their man from turning the ball toward goal.

• • •

Most of the teams at higher levels of competition play with two marking backs and a sweeper, therefore front players must defend against an extra player. At times they will have to work very hard. They can't defend all three opponents man-to-man, of course, so teams must use combination man-to-man and zone marking.

If, for example, the opponent's right back has the ball, one of the forwards should be marking him while the other forward covers their two other backs. Teams want to encourage the opponent to make square passes, so the tar side (away from the ball) forward should be withdrawn in case the opponent's backs should decide to come forward.

As a general principle, leave the far side — the weak side — of the field open. If the ball is in the center, controlled by the opponent's two central defenders, the forward withdraws and does not go forward to pressure the sweeper; that would leave open a pass to a marking back. The outside forwards must stay with the wing backs in this situation. If the opponent attacks with wing backs, a team's forwards must work extra hard to nullify the opponent's attack.

If the opponent uses its backs in attack, an option is to use one of the forwards as a chaser to keep pressure on the ball, and perhaps force the opponent's backs to one side of the field. The other forward tries to limit the passing opportunities between the opponent's other backs.

Another option is to send a midfielder forward to defend so that the opposing backs are all marked and have the other midfielders play a zone defense. This strategy gives the opponent a man advantage in the midfield. This is a good strategy to use when the opponent generates its attack out of the back and does not like to build through midfield. A third option would be to play without a sweeper by having the sweeper push up on their center striker and have everyone else mark up the opponent closest to him. If the opponent is very strong coming out of the back and a team wants to disturb the attacking rhythm, this strategy can accomplish that and change the momentum of the match.

• • •

Special attention must be given to weak side defense in practice. The biggest danger for an opposite-side defender is to be caught ball-watching and get blind-sided by players running behind him. Too many players lose concentration and become ball-watchers. They need to discipline themselves to watch the ball and still not lose sight of the man they are defending.

As a general principle, when the opposing team has possession on the right touch line, defenders must mark opponents tightly who are near the ball. The weak side defenders play more loosely, but not so loose that they can't intercept a pass when the point of attack is switched, or make a tackle when the ball is served in that direction.

• • •

Forced man marking exercises quickly reveal players who cheat defensively, because nobody can cover for them. We use forced marking as a teaching tool, such as in a three-on-three situation. We'll go with two- or three- minute bouts of hard transition work.

Teams should not neglect one-on-one defensive principles in training. At times it is wise to apply a restriction, such as no tackling. Too often, younger players want to commit and win the ball from an opponent when that is the last thing they should be thinking. An opponent with the ball has the advantage, and the defense must find ways to take that advantage away.

One-on-one exercises should be done between goals up to 30-40 yards apart, with goalies, and should end with an attempted shot on goal. Too many times these activities are done without a finish and the players forget about attempting to score. This has kept players in the United States a bit behind the rest of the world. Players should be conscious of scoring goals at all times.

• • •

One of the biggest weaknesses we find with new players joining the team concerns tackling. We work very hard on commitment. Unless a player is 100 percent sure of winning the ball, we don't want him to tackle. The good attackers are just waiting for a defender to attempt a tackle, to stick a leg out. Then they're gone.

Front players, of course, have a little more freedom in this regard, but players in the defensive half of the field cannot take chances. They need to be patient and show restraint when confronting an attacker in possession of the ball.

We want our players to pressure the dribblers without committing and wait for doubleteam help from behind, or shepherd the ballhandler away from the danger zones. The minute a defender commits to a tackle and fails, the team is playing at a numerical disadvantage.

It's also difficult to teach players not to go for foot fakes when an attacker fakes a shot or pass. A lot of times defenders have their eyes focused on the opponent and not the ball, and we have to work hard defensively to get our players to react only to the ball.

Learning how to properly run backward also is an often-overlooked, yet important technique in defense, as is knowing how to turn properly using the shortest radius. If a player needs to improve his ability to run backward, we'll have him practice marking a moving attacker. The exercise progresses into a more match-related setting by adding extra players and two goals.

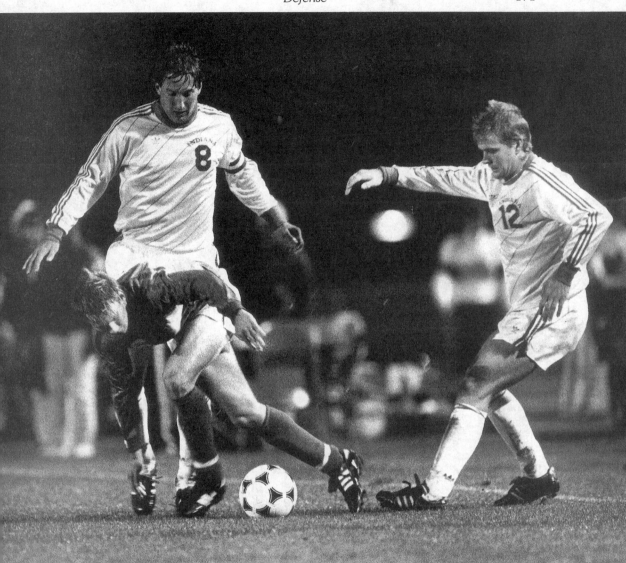

• • •

We don't use the offside trap defensively, because it takes a great deal of understanding and communication. The professional teams that play together day after day and year after year can do it, but it's not practical for college teams or younger teams. Even if a team executes the trap perfectly, all it takes is for one linesperson not to catch it. Most teams that utilize the offside trap a great deal get burned, either by poor communication or by poor officiating.

15

Restarts

Restarts, or set plays from free kicks, corner kicks and throw-ins, are often overlooked when determining soccer strategy. Yet it has been estimated that nearly 40 percent of all goals are scored directly or indirectly from set plays. The more evenly matched the teams are in a game, the more likely it is that execution of set plays will determine the outcome of the game.

Our national championship in 1982 was largely the result of executing restarts. Our first goal in a 2-1 eight-overtime victory came when Gregg Thompson scored off of a throw-in. Our second goal came off of a free kick by Thompson.

Set plays present excellent scoring opportunities when executed in the attacking third of the field for several reasons, including the following:

- Specific plays can be rehearsed many times during practice to maximize timing and each player's technical abilities.
- Several attacking players, as many as nine, can be involved in the play in a concentrated area.
- The defenders must be at least 10 yards from the ball on free kicks and corner kicks, leaving the kicker with an unobstructed opportunity to accurately serve the ball.
- The play always is initiated with a still ball, which helps ensure accuracy.

Coaches should resist the temptation to install multiple play combinations for restarts. It is better to be able to execute a few plays extremely well than it is to have many plays that have not been mastered. Even if the opponent knows what a team plans to do on a restart, it is difficult to stop if it executes well.

Set plays pose a challenge for coaches during practice. They are time-consuming and they involve little activity, so the players are standing around for a substantial period of time. Players can become bored and lose concentration.

We have our restart specialists work on their own before or after practice each day, and then work on restarts with all the field players involved for 10-15 minutes at the end of practice. We also practice restarts within a full-sided scrimmage occasionally by calling fouls that did not occur to practice free kicks, or setting up corner kicks as we see fit. We also might work on corner kicks at the end of practice, taking 10 from each side of the field against a full defense.

Throw-ins

The throw-in is the most common of all restarts — each team takes up to 60 each game — and for that reason alone it merits special attention from a strategic standpoint. It can be much more than a simple method of putting the ball into play when well executed.

Defensive players often relax and lose concentration when throw-ins are taken, probably because the play often appears inconsequential. This provides an excellent opportunity for an attacking team that has a well- practiced strategy.

The most fundamental strategy for the attacking team regarding throw-ins is to make the play quickly. Defensive players who are tired or simply lack concentration are likely to be resting during this break, and they can be exploited. Therefore, the player closest to the ball should make the throw whenever possible. An exception would occur when the team's best long thrower is needed to initiate the play in the attacking third of the field.

The throws generally should be made to whichever player happens to be unmarked, because that player can best advance the ball and start the attack. This requires quick thought and action on the part of the thrower, as well as his teammates.

If at all possible, the throw should be made forward toward the opposing team's goal. This forces defenses to make recovery runs, and creates a potential scoring opportunity. If no opening exists in that direction, however, the ball should be thrown back to an unmarked player. That player can then look to move the ball forward.

The player making the throw should recognize that he is making a pass, just as he does on the field of play, but with his hands instead of his feet. The ball should be thrown into an area and at a pace that enables the receiving player to make a constructive play. If the receiving player is to head the ball back to the thrower, for example, the ball should be thrown at the receiving player's chest, which would allow him to head through the top half of the ball back to the thrower's feet.

The thrower also should make it a point to become part of the offense as soon as he inbounds the ball, rather than standing on the touch line and watching. He can try to support the player with the ball and create a numerical advantage in that area, or make a run to draw the defense and create an opportunity for a teammate.

The receiving players should be careful not to set up too close to the thrower, or to each other. By spreading out, they create more offensive opportunities and make it more difficult for the defenders to mark them.

The strategy for throw-ins also depends on the part of the field from which the throw-in is made and the strength of the thrower. Teams throwing from the defensive third of the field should play it safe; retaining possession is the most important thing. The ball should not be thrown to the center of the field unless a teammate is wide open. If possession is lost, it can set up an immediate scoring opportunity for the opposing team.

Teams throwing from the middle of the field can afford to take slightly greater risks in moving the ball forward, although they still must emphasize retaining possession. Tactics such as switching and dummy runs are an effective means of setting up a positive attacking play. Players running to receive the ball should make sharp runs and cuts to create openings.

In the offensive third of the field, teams can take greater risks in trying to set up a scoring play. Throw-ins from this area of the field are similar to free kicks and corner kicks.

The ball can be thrown near the goal to create a quick scoring opportunity, perhaps even a one-touch strike. In this area of the field, getting the ball in quickly to catch the defense off guard takes on greater importance. The player nearest the ball should make the throw, and look for a penetrating pass. Teams cannot be offside on throw-ins, so a pass beyond the defense to an attacking player running toward the goal can be particularly effective.

Substantial practice time should be devoted to throw-ins, particularly from the attacking third. A team's strongest and most accurate throwers should be identified during practice so it is clear who should make the throws during games, when possible. The most effective throws are low, flat and hard, so that the receiving player can play the ball more effectively.

If a team is in the attacking third of the field, and it has a player capable of throwing the ball into the six-yard area, a long throw can set up an immediate scoring opportunity. The ball should be thrown with a low trajectory to the near post area. Ideally, a tall player will be in that area to head the ball into the goal or slip a pass to a teammate. Other teammates should make sharp runs to the goal area to play balls that get through to their attacking space. The timing of the support runs is crucial in making this play a success.

• • •

The most important factor in defending throw-ins is to get prepared quickly. Alert attacking teams will play the ball quickly, so the defense must not use this time to rest.

Overall, the basic principles of defense apply to throw-ins. It is important to mark all possible receivers, and then pressure the ball after it is thrown. Someone also must mark the thrower, so that he cannot run inbounds and receive a return pass without defensive pressure.

Teams at higher levels have players capable of throwing the ball into the six-yard area. These instances require special defensive attention. The defenders should shut off as much space as possible in the penalty area. They can position players in front of or behind the player receiving the throw, if not both, and position the goalkeeper in the front half of the goal.

Direct free kicks

Direct free kicks offer excellent scoring opportunities when taken from inside the 'D' (the arc at the top of the penalty area) or from favorable angles. They should not be taken lightly.

When taking kicks from this area, the attacking team can be sure that the defenders will form a wall to protect a portion of the goal from the driven shot. The goalkeeper, meanwhile, will stand off to one side so that he can see the ball's flight and protect the part of the goal not blocked by the players forming the wall.

Attacking strategy, therefore, should focus on screening the goalkeeper's view of the ball to make it more difficult for him to save the shot, whether it is driven or chipped.

The most common and effective method of accomplishing this is to place players from the attacking team near the defenders' wall, thereby blocking the goalkeeper's view. These two or three players should be placed less than 10 yards from the ball, two or three yards closer to the kicker than the defending players. This prevents them from being offside, and enables them to obscure more of the goal then they could at a greater distance. It also makes them available to score off of rebounds.

The attackers should stand close together, with their feet closed, so that the goalkeeper does not have a "window" to look through. They also should break after the ball has been kicked; however, if they leave too early, they allow the goalkeeper to pick up the ball's flight more easily. They should converge on the goal from opposite sides in case they have an opportunity to play a rebound.

We like to assign the people who take our free kicks rather than have whoever is closest to the ball make the kick. When we get in position to score on a free kick, we want to take full advantage of the opportunity by having specialists kick the ball. Unless a team has someone who can serve the ball with proper pace and accuracy, chances of success are diminished. Teams are just kicking a ball into the mixer and hoping for the best otherwise.

It is common strategy to have two or three players line up to make the kick. This helps place the defensive players off-balance. They don't know which player will kick the ball, and the player who does not make the kick helps screen the goalkeeper's view.

The two potential kickers should approach the ball from opposite angles at a brisk pace. Ideally, one of the players would be right- footed and the other left-footed. They will have decided before approaching the ball who should kick the ball and what type of kick should be made. The player not making the kick should run slightly in front of the ball to further block the goalkeeper's view, and should continue toward the goal to play a possible rebound. The first player to reach the ball can make the kick, too, however.

Three basic shots are available to the kicker:

- A drive through the attacker's portion of the wall
- A bending shot around the outside of the wall
- A bending shot over the wall

The sharper the angle from which the kick is taken, the fewer options available to the attacking team. It generally is best to play the ball to the back of the defense — preferably to the near post, and preferably with a bending kick. To accomplish this, a kick from the right side of the field should be taken by a left-footed player, and a kick from the left side of the field should be taken by a right-footed player.

With free kicks around midfield, where we don't have a realistic scoring opportunity, we like to put the ball into play as quickly as possible to try to catch the defense unaware, just as in the case of throw-ins.

• • •

Defending against free kicks near or inside the penalty area requires a team to set up a wall. This is a necessary evil of set play defense in the attacking third of the field; without it, the attacking team would have a clear shot at the goal. But it places the defense at an extreme numerical disadvantage, so all defensive players must execute their jobs properly.

One player must be designated to set up the wall. It can be a goalkeeper or a field player. In either case, this must be worked out in practice to avoid confusion during games. At Indiana, we use a field player.

If a field player is in charge of lining up the wall, he should stand out field approximately 10 yards from the wall and in line with the goal post with which the wall is to be set. If the kick is taken from a wide angle, the wall should be set on the outside of the near post to make a driven shot more difficult. If the kick is taken from a more central position, the wall should be set up according to the goalkeeper's preferences, which should be established during practice.

The only player who needs to be positioned is the one outside of the wall. He should be in a direct line between the ball and the post, 10 yards from the ball. The rest of the players forming the wall line up next to him.

The number of players used to form the wall depends on where the kick is made from (see chart on next page). Generally, the more central the position of the kick, the more players needed in the wall. If the kick is made from the 'D', as many as five players should be used to form the wall. If the kick is made between the 'D' and the corner of the penalty area, three to five players should be used. If the kick is made from near the side of the penalty area, one or two players should be used.

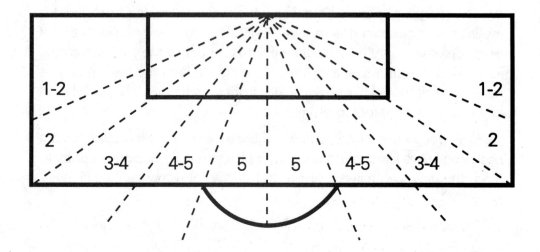

The closer to the touch lines or to the defending third of the field the kick is taken from, the fewer the number of players required to form the wall. In some instances, only one might be needed.

Teams should be prepared so that they know how many players to use in forming a wall under any circumstance. The goalkeeper, or another player, can shout the number to help maintain order. Players need to know ahead of time who will be used for the wall, and where they should stand. Ideally, a team's best defenders should not be in the wall; they will be needed to mark attacking players after the ball is put into play. At the same time, the wall must have courageous players willing to take a hard-kicked ball to the body.

The players should stand close together, with their feet less than a foot apart, so that the ball cannot be kicked between them or through their legs. The tallest player should stand on the outside of the wall, and the shortest on the inside. In instances where three or more players are forming the wall, one player should stand outside the player lined up with the near post to defend against bending shots around the wall. The goalkeeper usually takes a position on the far post side of the goal line.

Occasionally players forming the wall link arms or put their arms around each other's waists. This is not recommended, because the players are not able to protect themselves from the force of the kick, and their movement after the kick is restricted.

The players forming the wall should protect themselves as much as possible by crossing their hands in front of their lower abdomen and groin area and lowering their heads slightly so that ball does not hit them directly in the face. At the same time they must stand tall and not leave their feet or turn their backs to a hard-driven shot.

The players should break from their positions *after* the ball is kicked. It is better to break too late than too early, because an early break could create an opening for the kicker. It generally is best for the players in the wall to move together toward the ball after it is kicked, to increase their chances of blocking a subsequent shot on goal.

The placement of the defensive players away from the wall also is vitally important. All of them should be used; the scoring opportunity for the attacking team is too great not to take advantage of all available resources.

The position of these players depends on the placement of the ball before it is kicked. When the kick is made from inside the 'D', the defense must guard the area of the field between the six-yard area and the penalty area.

Indirect free kicks

Indirect free kicks, when taken within the 'D', are similar to free kicks taken from the same area. The difference is that the kicker cannot take a direct shot on goal; he must play it to a teammate first. Therefore, a slight adjustment must be made in the placement of the attacking wall.

Indirect kicks from inside the penalty area are rare, but teams must be prepared for them. The defense probably will place all 11 players inside the goal area, or on the goal line if the kick is taken within 10 yards of the goal.

If the ball is positioned at a sharp angle from the goal, the first touch should be made with the purpose of widening the angle. If necessary, the ball should be played backward, to improve the angle and provide more time for the shot on goal. The shot should be taken to an area opposite the position of the goalkeeper.

Indirect kicks taken outside the attacking third of the field should be taken as quickly as possible to take advantage of any lack of organization on the part of the defense. At least two players should move toward the ball quickly to enhance the speed and effectiveness of the play. Meanwhile, the players in advance of the ball should get behind their opponent.

Choreographed patterns are not needed in the non-attacking two-thirds of the field. Here, attacking teams should focus on getting the ball into play quickly and taking advantage of whatever openings the defense allows. The best approach is to use some degree of improvisation.

• • •

Defending indirect free kicks is much like defending direct kicks near the penalty area. The defense must be aware, however, that a direct shot toward the goal is unlikely unless the attacking team is hoping for a deflection into the goal, such as off the body or head of a player in the wall. More likely, a pass will be made first to change the angle of the shot.

The defense must try to cover as much of the goal as possible with a wall. In some cases, if the ball is placed close to the goal, all 11 players will be standing on the goal line within the goal posts. In these instances, the goalkeeper should stand in the middle of the wall.

After the first kick is taken, but before the second touch, the wall should converge on the ball. This better enables those players to prevent the shot and provides an opportunity to catch the attacking players offside.

Corner kicks

Corner kicks provide excellent scoring opportunities, particularly when two or more players combine to create a shot on goal, such as with a header. Most teams get about 10 corner kicks during a game, and each one offers a terrific scoring opportunity.

A team's strategy on corner kicks should depend on the individual strengths of its players. An accurate kicker is essential, of course. He must be able to serve the ball to an unmarked area of the goal, at an exact spot where it can be played by a teammate. Inswinging bending balls present the most difficulty to the defending team.

Teams that lack such a kicker — youth teams in particular — have other options available to them. They can take advantage of the 10- yard rule and make a short pass from the corner. The receiving player can then try to create a play, and often will have a two-on-one or three-on-two numerical advantage to try to exploit. More advanced teams should be prepared to make scoring attempts directly from the inbounding kick.

Generally, at least one player will be positioned on the far side of the goal, just outside the penalty area. This player, or players, should be one of the team's most skilled headers. He will make an angled run and attempt to meet the kicker's pass for a shot on goal, or nod the ball back to the near post for a teammate to shoot on goal.

Another player should be close to the far post, just outside the six-yard box. He is in position to make a short run toward goal, but also can go back to play a pass. Also, someone should be placed in the mid-goal area, and someone on the near post area of the goal from where the kick is made.

Most successful plays are made to the near post area, but not by a wide margin over other areas. Corner kicks to the near post area are more likely to be accurate because of the shorter distance, and they create many options for the receiving player. He can try to flick the ball into the goal with a one-touch maneuver, or play it to a teammate for a shot on goal. He also can come off the near post and take a short corner pass, then try to create a play by dribbling or passing.

A few corner kicks to the near post can be an effective means of setting up scoring opportunities in other areas. Because of the difficulty in defending the near post, defenses often concentrate on that area — which can leave an opening at mid-goal or at the far post.

Despite the various strategies available on corner kicks, attacking teams should leave themselves room for improvisation based on how the defense sets up. Players who are not designated to play in specific positions near the goal should line up according to what the defense leaves open, filling in where they will have the best opportunity to participate in the play. Blind-side runs are an effective means of creating scoring opportunities on corner kicks.

● ● ●

Because of the options available to the attacking team, defending corner kicks is a difficult task. The most important principles are to get enough bodies near the goal to give the defense a fair chance to stop the play, and to not get caught watching the ball.

The best setup ordinarily is to put all the midfielders and one or two forwards near the goal. It usually is best to leave one player near the halfway line in case a fastbreak opportunity arises. All players in attacking positions should be marked, and the goalkeeper should be provided plenty of support at the near and far posts.

Defense at the near post is particularly crucial, as many teams play the ball into that area. The defenders there must be prepared to cut off a bending serve and a hard low drive, to mark attackers in that area and to watch out for angled runs.

The position of the goalkeeper depends on what he perceives to be the tendencies of the attacking team, based on scouting. In years past it was common for the goalkeeper to play in the area of the far post, but as more teams focus on making corner kicks to the near post, the goalkeeper must adjust by playing at mid-goal or closer.

Communication is of the utmost importance for goalkeepers after the corner kick is made. He must make a clear, positive call to let his teammates know his intentions and avoid excess confusion in a situation that is chaotic by nature. Corner kicks often demand that the goalkeeper punch the ball out of the goal area, rather than trying to catch it.

Just as the attacking team must improvise according to the defensive play on corner kicks, the defenders must be prepared to adjust according to the alignment of the attacking team. The posts must be protected, but the rest of the goal area coverage must be flexible, depending on the what the offense does.

A cardinal rule for defenders on corner kicks is to play the ball aggressively. It does no good to have everyone in proper position if the defenders allow the attacking team to play the ball unchallenged. Because of the intense assault on its goal, it is natural for the defense to be in a somewhat passive state of mind, reluctant to make a play for the ball out of fear of leaving the goal unprotected. Defenders near the goal must challenge for the ball as aggressively as the attacking players.

Part III:
Fitness Training

16

Getting in Shape

The importance of fitness training in soccer should be readily apparent. No other team sport demands as much in terms of cardiovascular endurance and muscular strength. Yet many players and coaches fail to devote enough time and energy to achieving maximum physical condition.

Even the most skilled players are useless to their teams if they aren't in peak condition. Many times, the team that wins the close game in the final minutes is the one that is in the best physical condition. Fitness training also builds mental toughness and discipline that can carry over to game performance; likewise, lack of conditioning can lead to fatigue, which causes a loss of concentration and detracts from performance.

Today, the top players must be able to perform to the best of their abilities for at least 90 minutes. The "one-way" player no longer has a place. When in possession of the ball, every player must concentrate fully on attack. When the opposition has possession, every player must devote himself totally to defense.

We won our first national championship in a game that lasted eight overtimes. Our second championship was won in a game that went two overtimes. We obviously wouldn't have been able to win those titles if we had not been in excellent condition. Regardless of the level of competition, players are bound to participate in close games in which conditioning plays a major role in determining the winner.

Basic fitness training needs that must be met are as follows:

1. **Running endurance.** Soccer players must be able to run almost continuously for 90 minutes, at varying speeds.

2. **Speed.** Players must have that extra "gear" to accelerate past opponents.

3. **Strength.** Players need to be able to kick harder, throw farther, tackle more powerfully and jump higher than their opponents. Strength also helps prevent many injuries common to soccer.

4. **Muscular endurance.** Players must be able to use their strength over a long period of time while jumping, heading, dribbling, shooting, tackling, twisting, turning and changing direction continuously.

5. **Flexibility.** Players must have a complete range of motion to better execute their skills. Flexibility also helps avoid some injuries.

At the major college level, it is essential that the players devote ample time to fitness training during the off-season. Coaches simply cannot afford to spend a great deal of practice time on conditioning. Members of youth league teams, of course, cannot realistically be expected to follow an off-season fitness training program. High school players can, perhaps, to a lesser degree.

Regardless, if the players aren't already in shape, fitness training must become a major focus of practice. It should be approached gradually, however, so that players do not suffer injuries resulting from over-exertion.

Many coaches tend to shy away from fitness training because it's no fun, for them or the players. They want to improve their players' skills and they want their players to like them, so they are reluctant to devote much time to the "dirty work." That's a mistake, at least at the higher levels of play. However, fitness training can be incorporated into many training activities that also improve ball skills.

Players of all field positions require the same conditioning program, although goalkeepers merit a slight exception. Goalkeepers need to have endurance, but not in the same way as a player who has to run for 90 minutes. They require a more explosive type of conditioning, which can be achieved through activities such as taking a rapid succession of shots on goal for a designated period of time. There's no magical length of time, but 30-40 seconds is common.

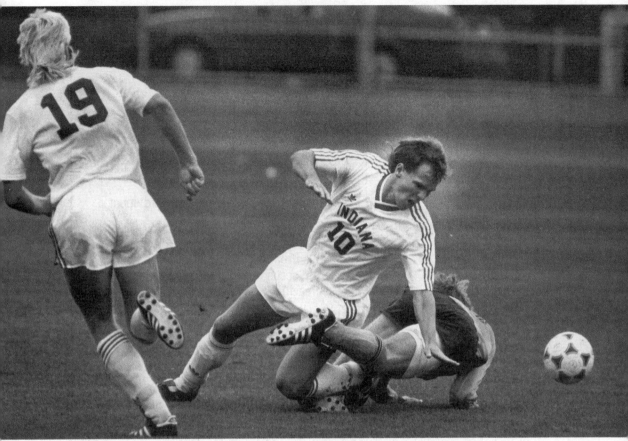

When I played high school and college soccer in the late 1950s and early 1960s, we did a lot of running without the ball to improve our fitness. My teams now do very little conditioning without the ball during the season. It is more efficient to incorporate running with specific skill activities.

Some coaches believe players must actually run sprints to achieve complete aerobic conditioning. The line of thinking here is that players cannot run as fast with the ball as they can without it, therefore they do not achieve the full conditioning benefit from practice activities. This is true, but running at full speed can be incorporated into practice in other ways. We get in a lot of sprinting while working on transition between offense and defense, for example. I don't believe you need to run up and down the field without a specific purpose.

During the off-season, however, players should follow a structured running program so that they report to practice in peak condition. The off-season running program our players use follows. It is designed to prepare them for the start of practice in mid-August, but it can be adapted to fit any team's schedule.

Off-Season Fitness Training Program

MONDAY	TUESDAY	WEDNESDAY
Stretch	Stretch	Stretch
Jog 1/2 mile	Jog 3 miles until July 15	Jog 3/4 mile
Stride to sprint 100 yards, 18 repetitions (30-second rest between each sprint)	660-yard sprint	Jog 4 miles between July 16-31
	Jog 5 miles between August 1-12	Jog 1/4 mile
Stride to sprint, 40 yards, 15 repetitions (15-second rest between each sprint)	Five 40-yard strides (30-second rest between each)	550-yard sprint
		Jog 1/4 mile
Jog 1/2 mile	Five 40-yard backward strides (30-second rest between each)	220-yard sprint
Restretch		Jog 1/4 mile
	Restretch or scrimmage	110-yard sprint
	Jog 1 1/2 mile	Jog 200 yards
		40-yard sprint
		Jog 1/2 mile
		Restretch

THURSDAY	FRIDAY	SATURDAY
Stretch	Stretch	Stretch
Jog 3 miles until July 15	Jog 1/2 mile	Jog 20-30 minutes
Run 80 yards, walk 20 yards (10 repetitions with no rest)	Restretch	
	Walk 1/4 mile	
Jog 5 miles between August 1-12	Run 40 yards, walk 15 yards (15 repetitions with no rest)	**SUNDAY**
		Rest!
Five 40-yard strides (30-second rest between each)	Backward sprints on level surface (50 yards backward, walk back to start; 8 repetitions)	
Five 40-yard backward strides (30-second rest between each)	Jog 1 1/2 miles	
Restretch or scrimmage		
Jog 1 1/2 mile		

• • •

A soccer player's sprinting ability is an important asset to his performance. Many occasions will arise during a game in which a player needs to get from one point to another at top speed. Therefore, improving one's speed can improve one's game.

To improve speed, concentrate on the following fitness components:

1. Increase stride length through flexibility and sprint drills.

2. Increase rate and efficiency of arm and leg movement. One must also relax and utilize best angles of motion.

3. Improve starting ability, both from a standing and crouched stance.

4. Increase endurance. This enables one to maintain rate of speed through sustained stride length.

5. Improve flexibility to utilize a full range of motion in the hips, lower back, shoulders and ankles.

6. Increase strength through hill running and weight training. Additional strength enhances explosive leg power and speed through greater stride length.

While running sprints, athletes should concentrate on lengthening the stride as much as possible without over-striding, and keeping the stride low to the ground without bounding. It also is important to run erect, staying up on the toes and holding the chest high.

At the same time, athletes should run as relaxed as possible. This enables them to move their arms and legs with maximum efficiency and speed, and minimizes fatigue.

Sprinting, of course, also enhances conditioning and stamina. Allow only enough rest between sprints to maintain proper form for each effort.

Sprints are most effective when performed over a distance of no more than 60 yards. This distance enables the athlete to maintain an emphasis on form and effort. It is best for the athlete to accelerate in a steady, relaxed manner for 20 yards, sprint for 20 to 50 yards, and then gradually decelerate for 20 yards.

The following exercises can be incorporated into speed work:

High knee. Run forward, lifting the knee until the thigh is parallel to the ground. When the right leg is lifted, the left leg should be pushing off the ground in a forward direction. The emphasis should be on form, and the drill should not be hurried. It is important to maintain correct upright body posture. The high knee lift action is sustained during the 20-yard action phase of the drill.

Plantar push. Emphasis is placed on speed and a strong plantar push. The down extended leg and foot is checked for a full response off the running surface as the opposite knee is fully lifted as rapidly as possible throughout the 20-yard action area

Leg reach. Lift the knee high, followed by a full extension of the foreleg. This action is an attempt to reach the maximum stride length. It is necessary to focus on balance, as the knee is fully lifted and the lower leg is thrust forward into the reaching position.

The arms also should reach forward (staying low) with each leg reach action. The arm that is back should not go behind the hip. Again, quality of form is emphasized, as speed is not as important as achieving a high knee lift and full extension of each lead leg.

Quick lift and reach. Utilize high knee action and leg reach action as rapidly as possible while maintaining proper form. More emphasis is placed on speed so that there is a greater carryover to race situations.

Relaxation. The focus of the high knee and leg reach action in this drill is on complete body relaxation. The jaw and facial muscles should be totally relaxed, and the arms and hands must be loose, but under control. This relaxation enables maximum speed of movement with a minimum loss of expended energy.

These exercises should be performed in sets of four, in the following order:

1. 4 sets of high knees
2. 4 sets of fast leg plantar push
3. 4 sets of leg reach
4. 4 sets of fast lift and reach
5. 4 sets of relaxation

• • •

Weight training has become more acceptable in recent years as a means of supplementing all sporting activities, including soccer. Some coaches have their players continue a full weight training program throughout the season, but we do not. Our players might lift some to maintain their strength during the season, and players who are particularly weak in one or two areas of the body will concentrate on those. But the primary part of our weight training program is done during the off-season.

Players should be working hard in their regular practice sessions, and they need to be fresh for the games. To lift weights in addition to their regular practice sessions might be too draining. Players should achieve peak condition during the off-season and then maintain most of that during the season.

Still, muscular strength is as important as aerobic fitness in performing at a peak level. Strength training stimulates circulation, helps maintain flexibility, increases appetite and neuromuscular control and enhances the sense of well-being.

The fundamental principles of a strength program should be as follows:

- Each exercise should work as much of the body as possible.
- Free weights should be used along with resistance machines.
- Consistency must be maintained. Strength training cannot be ignored for any long stretch of time. It should be part of a player's off-season workout schedule at least three days a week, on alternate days.

The time and energy invested in training, during the season and otherwise, should be maximized to its fullest. Athletes have neither the time nor energy to waste on ineffective or insufficient training methods.

A warm-up period should be an integral part of any workout schedule. Muscles cannot approach their maximum capability unless they are first properly loosened up by performing similar, less rigorous movements. An athlete cannot warm up properly for bench presses, for example, by performing standing presses. He must perform a set or more of bench presses with a resistance well below the maximum he can lift first.

A set is a series of repetitions. A repetition is one complete execution of an exercise. Studies indicate that muscular strength is best increased by performing five to eight repetitions per set. No more than three sets should be necessary for any exercise.

Before lifting, jog about one-half mile, then stretch. After completing the weight program, stretch again before performing any prescribed running or ball work.

A rest period of no more than two minutes should be taken between sets. All sets of a particular exercise should be performed in succession before beginning the next exercise.

Weight training tips

- Always warm up properly before lifting. This should include stretching for 10-15 minutes and jogging at least one-half mile.
- Proper technique is a must. Never sacrifice technique for added weight. Improper technique can lead to strength loss and injury.
- Be consistent. Progress will come only if an athlete works out regularly in a disciplined fashion.
- Progress systematically. An athlete should increase the weight by no more than 10 pounds after he is able to comfortably complete a set of the prescribed number of repetitions.

The following off-season strength program can be adapted to any team's schedule. Each phase should last three to four weeks. Younger players should not perform any exercise program without first consulting a doctor and a fitness expert.

A nearly endless variety of weight training exercises are available that can help improve a soccer player's performance. A sample routine and a description of the major exercises follows.

	Phase 1 (sets/reps)	Phase 2	Phase 3
MAJOR LIFTS			
Bench press	4×10	$4\text{-}5 \times 6$ 2×6 2×4	1×10
Squats	4×10	$4\text{-}5 \times 6$ 2×8 2×5	1×10
Power cleans	$4\text{-}5 \times 6$	$4\text{-}5 \times 4\text{-}5$	$4\text{-}8 \times 2\text{-}4$
Step-ups	$4 \times 8\text{-}10$	$5 \times 5\text{-}6$	$4 \times 8\text{-}12$
AUXILIARY LIFTS			
Leg curls	3×12	$4 \times 8\text{-}10$	3×15
Upright rows	3×12	$4 \times 6\text{-}8$	4×10
Side lunges	3×8	3×6	$3 \times 10\text{-}12$
Leg extensions	3×12	$4 \times 8\text{-}10$	3×15
Straight arm pulldowns	3×10	3×8	3×12
Toe raises	3×15	3×15	3×20
Manual neck resistance	2×10	2×10	3×10
Abdominal crunches	3×20	3×25	3×30

Bench press

Benefit: Overall development of the chest

Equipment: Bench and barbell, or bench press station

Procedure: Lie on your back on a flat bench with your legs positioned at each side of the bench with your feet flat on the floor. Grasp the bar with an overhand grip that is about six inches wider than shoulder width, then raise it to arms' length. Slowly lower the bar until it touches the middle of your chest. Inhale as you lower the bar. After the bar gently touches your chest, slowly lift it back to arms' length as you exhale.

Your buttocks and shoulders should remain on the bench at all times, and you should have only a slight arch in your lower back as you execute this exercise.

Caution: The bench press is dangerous because the bar can fall on you if it slips from your hands or if you cannot support the weight. You should have a spotter nearby, particularly when lifting weights close to your maximum capability, or use a safety rack, which enables you to crawl out from under the bar if it falls.

Squat

Benefit: Development of the lower back, hips and buttocks

Equipment: Barbell and squat rack

Procedure: Step under the bar on the rack and place it on your shoulders, stabilizing it with a comfortable grip. Keep your chin up, your back straight and your feet shoulder-width apart, with your toes pointed slightly outward. Inhale as you slowly lower your body until your thighs are parallel with the floor. Make your movement smoothly; do not bounce at any point. Keep your knees out over your toes. Stand up in a powerful motion, exhaling in the process. For added safety, you may squat over a flat bench, touching it with your buttocks at the bottom of your motion.

Caution: Be careful to use the proper technique to avoid possible injuries to your back or knees. Do not attempt this exercise with more weight than you are sure you can handle to avoid the risk of falling or dropping the bar. Do not bend lower than the prescribed position.

Leg curl

Benefit: Development of the hamstrings

Equipment: Leg curl station

Procedure: This exercise can be performed with weights attached to your feet, but it is much easier to execute with a machine designed for the purpose. Lie face down with your lower legs extending over the edge of the bench (your knees should be just off the pad) and the back of your ankles under the pads or weights. Hold on to the front of the machine or bench for support. Keeping your hips on the pad, slowly raise your lower leg as high as possible, touching the back of your buttocks if you can. Return slowly to the starting position.

Caution: This is a safe exercise. Be careful, however, not to lift your hips off the bench as you lift, and do not position yourself so that your legs hyperextend when in the starting position.

Toe raise

Benefit: Development of the calf muscles

Equipment: Raised platform and barbell, or machine station

Procedure: This exercise can be performed with a barbell and something to step onto, or at a machine designed for this purpose. Place the barbell on your shoulders, or step underneath the weights of the machine. Stand on the balls of your feet; your heels should not be touching the platform. Raise up on your toes as high as possible. Pause and slowly lower. Pointing your toes straight ahead works the main calf muscles. Pointing your toes outward works the inner calf muscles. Pointing your toes inward works the outer calf muscles.

Caution: This is a safe exercise. Be careful not to bounce as you lower the weight, and keep your knees straight.

Upright row

Benefit: Development of the upper back and shoulders

Equipment: Barbell or upright cable rowing station

Procedure: This exercise can be performed with a barbell, or on a machine with an upright rowing station. Grasp the barbell or handles with your palms facing inward and your hands about hip width apart. Stand erect with your arms extended downward. Pull the weight straight up almost to your chin, keeping it as close to your body as possible. Keep the elbows up and out as you reach the top of the movement. Pause and slowly lower the weight to the starting position.

Caution: This is a safe exercise. The only danger comes from dropping the barbell, or attempting to lift too much weight and injuring the back.

Side lunge

Benefit: Development of the thighs

Equipment: Barbell

Procedure: Place the barbell on your shoulders along the upper back. Your feet should be positioned close together, your chin up and your back straight. Inhale and step out at a 45-degree angle with one leg until your thigh is nearly parallel to the ground. Keep your stationary leg straight, bending the knee as little as possible. Exhale and step back to the starting position. Repeat the movement with the other leg. Alternate back and forth.

Caution: It is important to perform this exercise with proper technique. Perform the movements smoothly to avoid excess stress on the knees and back. Do not bounce at the end of the lunge, and do not dip too low.

Leg extension

Benefit: Development of the quadriceps and knees

Equipment: Leg extension machine

Procedure: This machine can be performed with weight attached to the feet, but it is better to use a machine designed for the purpose. Sit on a bench with the top of your ankles touching the pads, or with the weights attached. Position yourself so that the edge of the bench is against the backside of your knees. Hold on to the seat next to the hips. Keep your toes pulled upward toward your knees, exhale and raise the weight until your legs are fully extended. Pause, inhale and lower the weight slowly and under control to the starting position. Keep your upper body still during the exercise.

Caution: This exercise is safe. Be careful not to bounce the weight or hyperextend the knees after lifting.

Straight arm pulldown

Benefit: Development of the triceps

Equipment: High pulley or lat machine

Procedure: Grip the bar or handles about three feet apart, if possible. Step back from the machine so that your arms are extended in front of your head and are supporting the weights. Bend forward slightly at the waist, keep your elbows slightly bent and locked, inhale and pull the bar straight down to the top of your thighs. Keep your elbows locked throughout the movement. Return to the starting position and exhale.

Caution: This is a safe exercise. Be careful to stand correctly to avoid possible injury to the back.

Neck resistance

Benefit: Development of the neck muscles

Equipment: Neck machine station, or none

Procedure: This exercise can be performed at a machine designed for the purpose, or with nothing but your hands and arms. To perform it without a machine, sit on a flat bench with your back straight. Place both hands on your forehead and lay your head back as far as you can with your chin up. Resisting with your arms, push your head forward until your chin touches your chest. Make the movement on a six count. Reverse the movement with your hands on the back of your head, pushing your head backward. Also place your right palm against the right side of your head and resist, then switch hands and resist to your left side.

Caution: This is a safe exercise, particularly when performed without a machine. Be careful not to make a jerking motion with the neck, and do not attempt to push too much weight when using a machine.

Power clean

Benefit: Development of the hips, legs, lower back and buttocks

Equipment: Barbell

Procedure: Place the barbell on the ground and stand over it. Bend your knees to grab the bar, keeping your back straight, and focus your eyes on a line slightly above the floor. Straighten your knees, shrug your shoulders and pull with your arms, swinging the bar out in front of you and up until it is "racked" on your chest.

Caution: This is an advanced lift, and should only be attempted with the supervision of an experienced coach or trainer. The dangers include the possibility of back injuries, losing your balance and having the bar land on top of you or spraining a wrist.

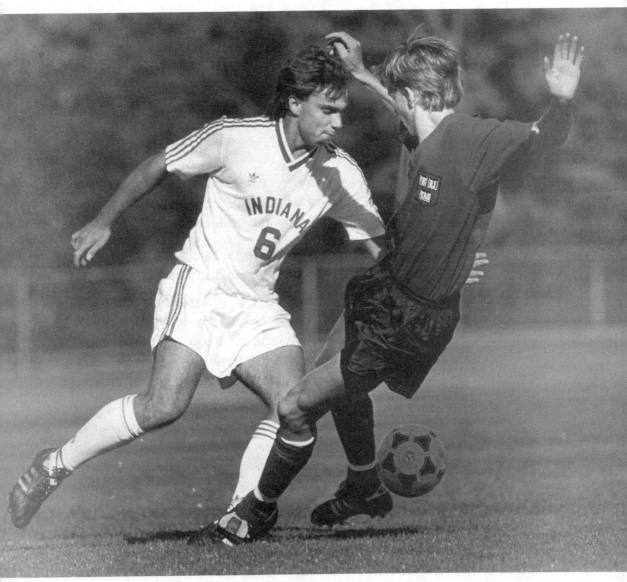

• • •

Stretching is an important part of fitness training that should not be overlooked. It used to be that players warmed up by performing ballistic stretching exercises and calisthenics, such as jumping jacks. Today the format is more sophisticated. We use an active stretching program that requires about 15 minutes each training session. It helps reduce many of the injuries that are common to soccer, such as groin pulls, and increases the players' flexibility.

Flexibility means a muscle can move through its entire range of motion easily and efficiently. Flexibility is somewhat determined by genetics; some athletes are naturally limber, while others are "stiff". All athletes can enhance their flexibility, however, through proper stretching.

Stretching your muscles achieves the following:

- Reduces the viscosity of muscular fluids
- Mobilizes blood reserves
- Generates heat in the muscle due to metabolism of contraction and relaxation, which enables the muscle to contract more powerfully
- Improves range of motion, which enhances nourishment of the joints

The end result is that the athlete will have greater dexterity, be better able to utilize his strength, and reduce his chances of injury.

An athlete should never force a stretch by bouncing on the muscle. This can cause an injury to the muscle, ligaments or cartilage. When a muscle is stretched too far, the body signals for a rapid contraction of the opposing muscle group (which is called a stretch reflex) and an injury can result. Usually an application of heat will relax the muscles and permit stretching, as will a basic warm- up routine such as jogging or light exercise.

When stretching, move the body or limb segment through its range of motion until you feel discomfort, but not pain. Maintain this position for 30 seconds, then release and repeat, each time trying to go a little closer to the full range. The stretching must occur gradually. It also helps to try contracting the opposite muscle group you are trying to stretch. For example, when stretching the hamstrings, contract the quadriceps.

To achieve maximum results, the athlete must start conditioning the muscles before the season begins. Proper training will substantially reduce muscle injuries, which generally occur when muscle fibers are stretched beyond their capability. A muscle that is unprepared for abnormal motion won't be able to withstand elongation.

• • •

The number of stretching exercises available is limited only by the number of muscles in the body and your imagination. Some basic exercises follow:

1. **Single knee to chest.** Bend your leg and pull your right knee to the chest, touching it to your forehead. Hold for 30 seconds, straighten leg, repeat for left leg.

2. **Straight leg pull.** Lay on your back and grasp the toes of your right foot with your right hand. Straighten your leg until your hip comes off the ground. Hold for 30 seconds. Repeat with left leg.

3. **Groin stretch.** From a sitting position, place the soles of your feet together and pull your heels as close to the buttocks as possible. With your hands on your ankles and elbows on your knees, push down with your elbows to try to get your legs flat on the ground. Hold for 30 seconds. Repeat.

4. **Ballerina.** Stand with your heels touching together and toes pointed outward. Bend over and touch the ground. Hold for 30 seconds without bouncing. Repeat.

5. **Hurdler's stretch.** Sit on the ground with your left leg stretched straight forward and your right leg bent so that the sole of the foot touches the inside of the left leg at the knee joint. Place your left hand on the floor or the ground at the left side. Reach forward with your right hand to touch your left toe. Hold for 30 seconds. Change leg positions and repeat.

6. **Stride stretch.** Stand on your left leg with the right leg extended parallel to the floor or ground. Place your hands on your hips then reach forward with both hands and try to touch the right foot. Hold for 30 seconds. Repeat with the opposite leg forward.

7. **Cross the tee.** Lay on your back with your arms perpendicular to your body. Swing your right leg high upward to touch your left hand. Hold for 30 seconds, then repeat on the opposite side.

8. **Straddle toe touch.** Sit with your legs outstretched at an angle. Lean forward and touch both feet with your hands (right hand to right foot, left hand to left foot). Hold for 30 seconds. Repeat.

Single knee to chest

Straight leg pull

Cross the tee

Indian seat

Groin stretch

Ballerina

Straddle toe touch

Straddle seat

9. **Straddle seat.** Spread your legs as far as possible and lean straight ahead, trying to touch your chest to the ground. Hold for 30 seconds. Repeat.

10. **Indian seat.** Sit on the floor or ground with your legs crossed at the ankles, Indian style. Put your hands behind your head with your elbows back, then lean forward and try to touch your forehead to your ankles. Do not put pressure on your head with your hands. Hold for 30 seconds. Repeat.

• • •

At Indiana University, we test our players' fitness and performance level three times a year to monitor their progress — upon their return to campus at the start of pre-season practice, upon the completion of the season and at the end of the academic year following the second semester training program.

Over the years, we have established norms and standards of performance. Players then can see how they compare to others, and hopefully are motivated to improve their performance level.

The testing items we use are as follows:

1. Two-mile run
2. Forty-yard dash
3. Bent leg sit-ups for one minute
4. Chin-ups
5. Standing broad jump
6. Vertical jump and reach
7. Obstacle dribbling
8. Kick for distance (stationary ball, with both feet)
9. Throw-in for distance
10. Head for distance
11. Kicking accuracy

• • •

Rest is as important to physical fitness as activity. Intensive processes of nutrition, food absorption and recovery of structural proteins and high-energy compounds take place in the organism during rest following intense activity.

The greater the intensity of the activity, the more extreme are the processes of recovery. If exercise is regularly repeated, body changes become firmly established and lead to growth of the working organs and to structural and functional perfection.

A normal training session should include breaks, as part of the recovery process takes place during these periods. Athletes should fill these intervals with a different kind of activity to speed recovery.

The fundamental part of the recovery process, however, takes place at night during sleep. Changes occur in the nerve cells of the core of the brain during this time, reducing the excitability of the centers which house various senses: hearing, sight, touch, and so on. Sleep calms the brain cells, replenishing their work capacity for the forthcoming activity of the organism.

Insufficient sleep causes the cells to become overloaded and leads to exhaustion. The amount of sleep required to replenish the body varies with each individual, but eight hours is adequate for most people.

• • •

Mental fitness is nearly as important to reaching your potential as a soccer player as physical fitness. Each player should develop a positive attitude toward his teammates, his coaches, the opponents, the laws of the game, the officials who enforce those laws, and most important, himself.

Only positive, constructive comments should be allowed between players. Negative comments and gestures quickly destroy player relationships and lead to the deterioration of team morale. Likewise, only positive comments should be directed toward an official by a player. Giving the proper respect to the laws of the game and the officials pays dividends in the long run. If a team cannot win within the framework of the rules, then victory is worthless.

Opponents are to be respected, and any intentional physical or verbal abuse should not be permitted. A rabid "kill the enemy" approach is counterproductive, because players need to address their full attention to their individual roles. At the same time, if a player becomes intimidated by the opposition, he loses concentration and becomes a much less effective team member.

Each player must feel good about himself and see himself as a worthy team member. He must be willing to work hard to prepare in order to achieve.

Following are some questions each player should be asked, or should ask himself, when trying out for a team.

1. What is your objective in soccer?
2. Are you willing to pay the price to find out how good you can be?
3. Are you willing to follow good personal habits relating to health and safety?
4. Are you willing to keep fit during the off-season?
5. Are you willing to work with your teammates toward a common goal?

If you have the desire to be the best and are willing to work toward excellence, you have the right attitude to be a part of a successful soccer program. The potential of your team depends directly on the potential of each player.

If every player trains and performs to the best of his ability, the team will be at its best. This is the ultimate anyone can hope for. Be proud. Don't settle for less than your best. This is the challenge. Are you willing and ready to accept it?

About the Author

Jerry Yeagley is the most successful collegiate soccer coach in the United States since 1973, when soccer became a varsity sport at Indiana University. Over the past 21 seasons, Yeagley's teams have won more NCAA Tournament games (36) and compiled a better overall record (359-65-32) than any other team in the country. Indiana won national championships under Yeagley in 1982, '83, and '88, has advanced to the Final Four nine times, and has appeared in the NCAA tournament 18 times. As a player, Yeagley was a member of the Myerstown (Pa.) High School state championship team and the West Chester State (Pa.) NCAA Division I championship team.

Yeagley is the only two-time winner of the NCAA Division I Coach of the Year award. He also is a recipient of the prestigious Bill Jeffery Award for his unique contributions to college soccer, a member of the National Soccer Hall of Fame in Oneonta, N.Y., and a member of the Pennsylvania Athletic Hall of Fame in Carlisle, Pa.